Secrets of Ittō-ryū

Book One

The publisher gratefully acknowledges the generous support of
Ariko Sasamori of the Reigakudō Foundation, Tokyo, Japan

Secrets of Ittō-ryū

Book One

Junzō Sasamori

Original publication had no ISBN
ISBN: 4-88458-168-7 C3075 (1986 edition)
ISBN: 4-88458-270-8 C3075 (2013 edition)
ISBN: 979-8-9872421-0-0 (2023 English edition)

Printed by Kindle Direct Publishing, USA

This translation is dedicated to the memory of the Reverend
Sasamori Takemi, 17th Sōke of Ono-ha Ittō-ryū

CONTENTS

CONVENTIONS

Japanese terms have been Romanized according to the Hepburn system and italicized on their first appearance. Long vowels are denoted by macrons. Common Japanese terms and phrases that appear in the *New Oxford American Dictionary* are written without italics or macrons. Japanese and Chinese personal names are written in the order of surname followed by given name.

References include footnotes and endnotes. Footnotes are as they appear in the original Japanese text, whereas endnotes have been added by the translator for additional reference or context.

Principal Periods of Japanese History	
Nara	710-794
Heian	794-1185
Kamakura	1185-1333
Ashikaga (Muromachi)	1336-1573
Warring States (Sengoku)	1467-1568
Azuchi-Momoyama	1568-1600
Edo (Tokugawa)	1603-1867
Meiji	1868-1912

ACKNOWLEDGMENTS

This translation started many years ago when I first joined the Reigakudō, the Tokyo headquarters of Ono-ha Ittō-ryū, and learned there was a book that contained all of the "secrets" of the school available to the public. Naturally, I wanted to draw on this resource when practicing. Of course, you can't learn a martial art through reading a book, so my understanding of what was written inside kept pace with my weekly practice in Tokyo. Now, after nearly twenty years of experience, I feel confident enough to offer a translation of this book, long available within Japan, to the English-speaking world.

I didn't get to this point alone and have many people to thank who have assisted me with this endeavor. First and foremost, I would like to thank the late Sasamori Takemi, the 17th Sōke of Ono-ha Ittō-ryū, who not only demonstrated technical mastery of the intricacies of this martial art but who, perhaps more importantly, created a welcoming environment within his school that attracted a wide variety of people from all walks of life – even foreigners like me – to study and flourish. I will always be grateful to him for his leadership, friendship, and wise counsel both in and out of the dojo. His wife, Sasamori Ariko, graciously granted me the permission to provide this translation. I am both humbled and grateful for her confidence in my ability and only hope that I can live up to her expectations.

This book also would not have been possible without the guidance I received over the years from the remarkable instructors and students of the Reigakudō, both living and since passed, to include the current sōke, Yabuki Yūji. Without seniors who can teach this extraordinary art and fellow students to train with, there would be no growth. Indeed, there would be no Ono-ha Ittō-ryū to pass on to future generations.

I also owe a debt of gratitude to those who helped with the translation, editing, copyrighting, and overall proofreading of this book. Mamie Lee, my senpai in and out of class has been there from the beginning to patiently answer questions and share in the research. Kajikawa Akiko, Kume Mami, Kato Tomoko, and Eric Shahan provided invaluable insights into the more nuanced aspects of the translations, particularly the kanbun. Hyunah Gray and Hart Larrabee were vital in helping me navigate the complexities of Japan's copyright laws. Grigoris Miliaresis helped shape the final product into a readable document others could understand, and Chris Loew, as usual, provided outstanding support with editing the final manuscript.

Last but not least I would like to thank my wife, Samantha, and daughter, Kai Lee, for their unwavering support even as I made them a "budo widow" and "budo orphan" over all these years. I love you both.

While all of those mentioned above provided invaluable support to this endeavor, any and all mistakes are mine and mine alone.

KEY HISTORICAL FIGURES

Chiba Shūsaku: Studied Ittō-ryū under both Nakanishi Tsuguhiro and Nakanishi Tanetake; created Hokushin Ittō-ryū.

Honda Yoichi: Son of a samurai of the Hirosaki clan. He was baptized in Yokohama where he was studying in 1872 and worked as a missionary. He became the head of Too Gijuku in 1874 and founded The Church of Christ in Hirosaki, Japan in 1875. He was elected a member of the Aomori prefectural assembly in 1882 and later served in leadership positions in various Christian universities and associations in Japan.

Itō Ittōsai Kagehisa: Originally named Maehara Yagoro; founded Ittō-ryū after engaging in many duels throughout the end of the Warring States period.

Kanemaki Jisai: Started out as a student of Chujō-ryū under Toda Seigen; later created his own school called Kanemaki-ryu. First formal kenjutsu teacher of Itō Ittōsai. Rumored to have also taught Sasaki Kojirō, Miyamoto Musashi's arch rival.

Maehara Yagoro: Name of Itō Ittōsai Kagehisa at birth.

Mikogami Tenzen: Name of Ono Jirōemon Tadaaki at birth.

Nakanishi Tanesada: Was a student of Ono Jirōemon Tadakazu; opened an Ittō-ryū training hall in Edo and attracted many students. This school is now commonly referred to as the Nakanishi-ha Ittō-ryū.

Obata Kagenori: A Confucian scholar and retainer of the Takeda clan during the Warring States period, who later served the Tokugawa. Became well known throughout Japan for compiling the *Kōyō Gunkan*, a chronicle of the Takeda clan's military campaigns, and for founding the Kōshū-ryū Gungaku, a school of military arts and strategy. He was a strong influence on Yamaga Sokō.

Oda Nobunaga: One of the most influential figures in Japanese history and regarded as the first "Great Unifier" of Japan. His rule was followed by Toyotomi Hideyoshi and, finally, Tokugawa Ieyasu who completed Japan's unification process.

Ono Jirōemon Tadaaki: Original name was Mikogami Tenzen; inherited the school of Ittō-ryū from Itō Ittōsai Kagehisa.

Ono Zenki: Was working as a ferryman when he met Itō Ittōsai Kagehisa and challenged him to a duel. Was defeated, asked to become Ittōsai's student and was allowed to accompany Ittōsai on his travels. Was Ittōsai's top student until he was defeated by Ono Jirōemon Tadaaki.

Toda Seigen: Learned Chūjo-ryū from his father, Toda Nagaie, who originally learned while living under the patronage of the House of Yamazaki. Around the time Seigen was learning Chūjo-ryū, it also came to be called Toda-ryū. Seigen taught swordsmanship to Kanemaki Jisai.

Tokugawa Ieyasu: The first shogun of the Tokugawa Shogunate of Japan, which completed the unification of Japan in 1603, ushering in an era of lasting peace until the Meiji Restoration in 1868. He was one of the three "Great Unifiers" of Japan, along with

Oda Nobunaga and Toyotomi Hideyoshi. He recruited Ono Jirōemon Tadaaki to teach Ittō-ryū to his son Hidetada.

Tokugawa Hidetada: The second Tokugawa shogun to rule Japan (from 1605 until 1623). He was the third son of Tokugawa Ieyasu and a student of Ono Jirōemon Tadaaki.

Toyotomi Hideyori: Son and designated successor of Toyotomi Hideyoshi.

Toyotomi Hideyoshi: Feudal lord (daimyo) of the late Warring States period regarded as the second Great Unifier of Japan.

Tsugaru Nobuhisa: The fifth-generation daimyo of the Tsugaru Domain; mastered the inner secrets of Ittō-ryū from Ono Jirōemon Tadao and inherited the system of Ittō-ryū as his sole successor.

Tsugaru Nobumasa: The fourth-generation daimyo of the Tsugaru Domain; mastered the secrets of Ittō-ryū from Ono Jirōemon Tadao and was noted for his accomplishments in both the literary and martial arts.

Takano Sasaburō: Became famous throughout Japan's martial arts community from the Meiji to Showa eras as one of the co-founders of the modern sport of kendo. Takano studied Ittō-ryū, first under his grandfather and then later in life under other Ittō-ryū masters. Was recruited by Sasamori Junzō to be the head coach of the Waseda University kendo team.

Yagyū Munenori: Founder of the Edo branch of Yagyū Shinkage-ryū school of swordsmanship, which he learned from his father Yagyū "Sekishūsai" Muneyoshi. Along with Ono Jirōemon Tadaaki, provided kenjutsu instruction to the Tokugawa family.

Yamaga Sokō: Was a Confucian scholar and military strategist under the Tokugawa Shogunate. Popularized the idea that the samurai class should adopt the Confucian ideal of the "superior man," which became the foundation for the modern concept of bushido. Was exiled to the Akō Domain by Hoshina Masayuki. Was taught Ono-ha Ittō-ryū by Obata Kagenori.

Yamaoka Tesshū: Was active from the final days of the Tokugawa regime until the early Meiji Era as a master swordsman and high-ranking government adviser. Studied Ono-ha Ittō-ryū under Asari Yoshiaki and Ono Nario; created his own school which he named Ittō Shōden Mutō-ryū.

MAP OF JAPAN

FOREWORD BY YABUKI YŪJI, 18TH SŌKE OF ONO-HA ITTŌ-RYŪ

As the heir of Ittō-ryū, I want to express my gratitude for the translation of this book, *Secrets of Ittō-ryū*, by Mr. Mark Hague.

Ittō-ryū is the quintessential school of Japanese swordsmanship, and its philosophy and spirituality are the foundations of bushido. My late teacher, Sasamori Takemi, the 17th Sōke of Ono-ha Ittō-ryū, made bushido the center of his life's work of contributing to world peace by applying the philosophy of Ittō-ryū together with the teachings of God. No one would be more pleased than Master Takemi to see the *Secrets of Ittō-ryū*, a manual on the spirit of bushido that formed the bedrock of his life, presented to the entire world.

The translator trained in Ittō-ryū for twenty years as a direct student of Master Takemi while serving in the U.S. military, and even after he retired from active duty, he moved to Japan and still earnestly studies Ittō-ryū today.

As an actual practitioner, the translator didn't just render words on paper, but parsed each and every lesson, learned their applications, and imbued them in his training, and the result, this book, no doubt will be embraced by those who love the martial arts the world over.

It is my hope that this book will assist martial artists around the world in their quest for self-improvement.

Yabuki Yūji
18th Sōke
Ono-ha Ittō-ryū

TRANSLATOR'S FOREWORD

English speakers who have heard of Sasamori Junzō, the author of this book, likely were introduced to him through his book, *This is Kendo, the Art of Japanese Fencing,*[1] which he co-authored with Gordon Warner in 1964. This was one of the first books on the sport of kendo ever written in the English language and has been the inspiration for countless non-Japanese to begin their martial arts journey, particularly in the sport of kendo.[2] What many outside of Japan (and many inside as well) don't realize, however, is how rich and varied the author's life was.

Sasamori Junzō was born into a samurai family on May 18, 1886 in Wakadochō, Hirosaki City as the youngest of six sons. This was only ten years after Japan's Meiji government banned the wearing of swords, which for all intents abolished the samurai as a class. His father, Yozo, was an expert with the spear as well as in gunnery and served as the Chief Master-at-Arms for the Tsugaru Domain. While the Lord of Tsugaru traveled to the capital of Edo during the period of social upheaval that accompanied the end of Edo period, Yozo went along as the head of his Household Guards detachment. Yozo was easily recognizable, as he was always garbed in a French-style military uniform with an impressive belt buckle adorned with the Sasamori family crest.

Kendo eighth dan, journalist, educator, statesman, and martial arts hero to many in Japan – Sasamori Junzō was one of Japan's most gifted post-war polymaths.

Junzō's father, mother, aunts, and uncles had all grown up as samurai of the Tsugaru Domain in the far north of Japan's main island of Honshu, so Junzō was steeped in the values of this warrior class from early childhood. At the age of six or seven, he entered the Hokushindō, one of the four main martial arts schools in Hirosaki, and started learning Ono-ha Ittō-ryū kenjutsu under the tutelage of Tsushima Kenpachi, the former official kenjutsu instructor of the Tsugaru Domain.

He continued his training when he entered Aomori Prefecture Number 1 Middle School. He joined the school's kendo club while continuing to practice Ono-ha Ittō-ryū under the guidance of Nakahata Hidegoro. Nakahata was a contemporary of kendo legend Takano Sasaburō, who often traveled to Hirosaki to train with him. It was through Nakahata that Junzō was first introduced to Takano.

After graduating from middle school, Junzō moved to Tokyo with the ambition of one day becoming a politician. He lived at a dormitory for students from Aomori Prefecture in Koishikawa while he continued his studies. In 1906, he was accepted into Waseda Preparatory High School and later entered Waseda University's Department of Political Economics.

Nakahata Hidegoro and Takano Sasaburō training together in Hirosaki.

While excelling in his studies, he also joined the university kendo club, where he distinguished himself in 1908 by taking first place in the All-Japan Young Men's Kendo Tournament. He was promoted to captain of the university kendo team, a position typically reserved for the most skilled practitioner. Shortly before his graduation, the club kendo coach decided to retire, and Junzō called on his kendo and Ono-ha Ittō-ryū senior Takano Sasaburō and encouraged him to take the position. Takano accepted and started as the head coach of the Waseda University kendo team in 1909. Shortly thereafter, Takano formalized his thoughts on kendo teaching pedagogy and published his first book on the sport, *Kendo*.

Junzō didn't get a chance to formally train under Takano, though, since Takano accepted the position in Waseda after Junzō had graduated, but he did maintain a lasting relationship with him. Takano and Junzō appeared as training partners in various martial arts demonstrations in Japan up until the 1940s.

After graduating from Waseda, Junzō took a job as a cub reporter at the *Shin Koron* magazine. At first, he did interviews and collected material for stories but was promoted to editor in chief after a year.

In 1912, he took the advice of his older brother who had lived and studied in the U.S. and decided to experience life in America. He headed to Seattle as his first stop and reportedly carried fifty bamboo practice swords and other training gear with him to pass to first-generation Japanese-Americans there so they could practice kendo.

Junzō, front row with moustache, in front of the Japanese M.E. Church in Denver, CO.

He eventually made his way to Denver, Colorado, where he worked as a reporter for a local paper that catered to the Japanese-American immigrant community. He also pursued a Master's Degree in the University of Denver, which he earned in 1915 (he eventually earned his Doctor of Philosophy in 1927 from the same school). While in Denver, he also visited fencing studios in the western United States, introducing the athletes there to Japanese martial arts. His activity in the U.S. made him one of the first pioneers to bring the sport of kendo to that country.

After a brief stint in California where he worked for another newspaper, Junzō eventually returned to Japan in 1922 to take up the position of Chancellor of the *Too-Gijuku*, a private high school in his home prefecture of Aomori. The *Too-Gijuku* had originally been the Tsugaru Domain's primary educational institute for young men from prominent samurai families but fell into disrepair after the start of the Meiji period. It was revitalized thanks to support from the United Methodist Church and converted into a Christian school, one of the few in Japan before World War II.

As Chancellor, Junzō implemented reforms he had brought with him from the U.S., such as abolishing entrance exams, replacing the traditional school uniforms with coats and ties, expelling students who failed to meet academic standards, and hiring foreign teachers, especially for foreign language courses. He also made kendo practice mandatory. This started a long and distinguished tradition of kendo within the school that persists to this day – the *Too-Gijuku* is considered a kendo powerhouse among high schools throughout Japan. He also invited other masters of martial arts to the school to teach kenjutsu, naginata, jujitsu and other forms of Japanese martial arts.

In 1926, after receiving the endorsement of the Tsugaru family, which maintained the main line of Ono-ha Ittō-ryū after the Ono family stopped teaching it, as well as receiving the full endorsement from the Yamaga family, which had acted as official martial arts instructors since the time of Ono Tadayoshi, Junzō brought both the Tsugaru and Yamaga lines together to become the 16th Sōke of Ono-ha Ittō-ryū. Around this same time, he also became headmaster of the Shinmusō Hayashizaki-ryū school of swordsmanship, and the Chokugen-ryū school of naginata.[3] Junzō was around forty years old when he assumed these roles.

In 1939, Junzō relocated to Tokyo and took up the post of Chancellor of *Aoyama Gakuin*, a Christian university in Tokyo. His tenure was short-lived, however, since he was subjected to harassment by Japan's military authorities, who were deeply suspicious of universities that accepted support from outside of Japan, as well as citizens, like Junzō, who had spent considerable time in foreign countries that were now allied against it. This harassment came to a head when the authorities threatened to send all of his young graduates to the front-lines as cannon fodder if he didn't step down. Seeing no way out, he resigned his position and left the school on June 30, 1943.

Thereafter, he went to work part time in the Greater East Asia Ministry, an offshoot of the Ministry of Foreign Affairs (MOFA) that was the focal point for policy concerning countries in Asia that fell under Japan's Greater East Asia Co-prosperity Sphere. Junzō worked there until the end of the war and transferred to the MOFA when the Greater East Asia Ministry was absorbed back into that ministry.

In 1945, Junzō returned to his hometown of Hirosaki, where, upon the urging of his previous fencing instructor and mentor, Yamaga Takatomo, he pursued his lifelong ambition of becoming a politician. He ran for a seat in Japan's national legislature and was elected to the Diet on April 10, 1946. One of his first duties in office was to serve as a Minister of State in the Katayama Cabinet, as the President of the De-mobilization Agency[4] from May 1947 until October of the same year, when it was disbanded, and then as the Director of the Repatriations Agency starting from its establishment on February 1, 1948.

First Katayama Cabinet. Junzō is second row, far right.

As a consequence of losing to the Allies in World War II, Japan was occupied by a foreign power for the first time in its history. U.S. and Allied forces under the command of General Douglas

MacArthur established a headquarters in the Dai-Ichi Seimei building in Marunouchi, the heart of Tokyo, and set about to remake Japanese society. From his perch in his General Headquarters – commonly referred to as *GHQ* – MacArthur and his staff dug into every sector of Japanese life, from its governmental and economic structures to its educational institutions, in an effort to replace its previous military dictatorship with a more pluralistic society that recognized civil liberties and the rule of law, and operated under a representative government that was ultimately accountable to the Japanese people.

GHQ's Civil Information Education (CIE) Section was charged with the task of reforming Japan's education system, which played a large role in indoctrinating children into supporting Japan's militarism during the war. GHQ concluded that one of the tools of this indoctrination was the practice of martial arts such as kendo and naginata, so they issued orders banning these activities in secondary and higher educational institutions. Once these orders were issued, high schools and colleges began to get rid of their kendo and other martial arts gear and repurpose their training halls for other activities.

Though not all institutions in Japan stopped practicing kendo – some local police precincts and private companies continued to operate schools, albeit out of sight – educational institutions couldn't escape the scrutiny of GHQ. They had no choice but to comply. Junzō, as an elected official and member of the Cabinet, became one of the strongest advocates within the Japanese government to persuade GHQ to rescind the ban. He argued that the martial arts were never about killing but were about personal development and growth, and removing them from the public school system would deprive educators of the very tools they needed to shape the character of a new generation of citizens.

Facemask that was part of the protective gear used in the sport of Shinai Kyougi

He was not immediately successful, nor was he the only one advocating GHQ overturn the ban, however, he ultimately gained the respect of the Japanese martial arts community for his willingness to stand up for the honor and integrity of the martial arts of Japan against the powerful occupiers. Ultimately, post-war kendo athletes were able to establish a work-around in the form of a Westernized style of kendo called *Shinai Kyougi*, literally *pliant stick competition*, in which players wore western-style fencing gear and followed toned-down rules. Junzō was elected chairman of this group in 1950. The Ministry of Education accepted Shinai Kyougi as part of the educational curriculum on April 10, 1952, the same year the U.S. occupation ended.

Shortly thereafter, Junzō was hired to work as an advisor on the movie *Seven Samurai*, along with martial arts master Sugino Yoshio of the Tenshin Shōden Katori Shintō-ryū. During production, however, the Ministry of Education asked Junzō to accept a mission involving overseas travel, and he ended up leaving the set without completing the movie, but his influence can be seen in scenes that reflect legends within the history of Ittō-ryū.

In 1956, Junzō invited Dr. Gordon Warner to Japan to participate in a Goodwill Kendo Tournament in Yokohama. Dr.

Warner was then an assistant professor at California State University, Long Beach, and was also a Marine veteran who had fought in the Pacific. One year later, Junzō toured the U.S. with a thirteen-man all-Japan university team to perform exhibition matches, with Dr. Warner's Long Beach State College as the site of the final match.[5] After this trip, he and Warner formed a lasting friendship that would ultimately see them publish a book together.

Komaba Eden Church and signboard for the Reigakudō, which stands outside the church's entrance.

Also, in November of the same year, Junzō established the Reigakudō Dojo (martial arts school) in his home in Komaba, in the Daizawa Ward of Tokyo. There, he taught Ono-ha Ittō-ryū, Shinmusō Hayashizaki-ryū, and Chokugen-ryū naginata. The school became not only the new headquarters for instruction in these traditions, but also a research center where Junzō continued to collect material on Japanese martial arts, particularly on the history of Ono-ha Ittō-ryū. His studies culminated in 1965 with the publication of this book, which represents over seventy years of practice and painstaking study of not only the physical techniques but also the philosophical background and history of this 400-year-old art.

Junzō had three sons and two daughters. His eldest son died while very young, while his eldest daughter died in her twenties. His middle son became a professional musician, while his youngest son, Takemi, moved to the U.S. after his undergraduate studies to attend seminary at Duke University. After graduating from Duke, Takemi became an ordained Methodist minister and spent a decade preaching in the U.S.[6]

Junzō founded the Komaba Eden Church in 1969 and co-located it with his martial arts dojo in his home, making it perhaps the only martial arts dojo-cum-Christian church in all of Japan. When his son Takemi returned to Japan the same year, he became the first pastor of the church. The Komaba Eden Church and Reigakudō Dojo continue to co-exist in the same location to this day, serving as both a place of worship and martial arts training center for parishioners and students alike.

Junzō demonstrating Ono-ha Ittō-ryū.

After serving as a reporter, both in Japan and the U.S., a chancellor of two different educational institutions, a statesman for over twenty years, founder of a Christian church, an accomplished martial artist in the sport of kendo, as well as headmaster of three ancient martial arts traditions, Junzō passed away on February 13, 1976. He was succeeded in his duties as head of the Komaba Eden Church and the Reigakudō Dojo by his son Takemi, who also succeeded him as the headmaster of Ono-ha Ittō-ryū, Shinmusō Hayashizaki-ryū, and Chokugen-ryū.

As you will read in the following chapters, Ittō-ryū has its roots in Chujō-ryū, which is one of the three primordial sword traditions of medieval Japan. As such, it is one of the most influential martial arts in Japan's history. This book, *Secrets of Ittō-ryū*, is the culmination of Junzō's lifetime of research into the history, techniques, and philosophy of the art. It is actually five books in one:

 The first book contains a brief history of Ittō-ryū, tracing its roots to Nen Ami Jion and the Chujō-ryū started by Jion's student, Chujō Hyogonosuke Nagahide. Junzō then details the lives of Itō Ittōsai Kagehisa and Ono Jirōemon Tadaaki and traces the evolution of Ittō-ryū as it migrated from the ancient capital of Edo to the city of Hirosaki and then back to Tokyo. In the course of this history, he introduces a who's-who of Japanese historical figures: Oda Nobunaga and Tokugawa Ieyasu, two of the greatest generals in the history of Japan; Yagyū Munenori, master of the Shinkage-ryū school of kenjutsu and fellow instructor to the Tokugawa; Obata Kanbei Kagenori, author of the *Kōyō Gunkan* and founder of the Kōshū-ryū school of military strategy; Yamaga Sokō, Confucian scholar, philosopher, and military strategist whose writings formed the intellectual foundation of bushido; Yamaoka Tesshū, sword master and senior government adviser credited with saving Edo from destruction during the Boshin War, and others.

 The second book provides a brief overview of how to approach practice, and then provides a detailed, step-by-step guide to the kumitachi, the vast collection of pre-arranged patterns and moves that comprise the curriculum of Ono-ha

Ittō-ryū. Ittō-ryū has over 170 "moves," which are two-person, pre-arranged patterns performed with the wooden sword or steel sword with a blunted edge. These moves are grouped together into sets of pre-arranged movements called "kata" and given names, such as the Odachi kata, Kodachi kata, Aikodachi kata, etc. This second book provides detailed descriptions of how to do these moves and how they instantiate the more esoteric principles of the school.

⊖ The third book provides advice and guidance on how to improve in the modern sport of kendo.

⊖ The fourth book introduces the transmission documents and licenses; [7] scrolls that list the philosophical and technical principles that are the heart of the school. In theory at least, these principles are the "secret sauce" that drive and animate the moves executed in the kumitachi. One can practice the kumitachi over and over for many years, but if one doesn't understand how the movements in them pertain to the theories and principles in these documents, practice becomes an empty activity. In fact, in the past, the information in these scrolls was considered a state secret that could have warranted the death penalty to those who leaked them to outsiders.

⊖ Not all the secrets of the school are recorded in the transmission documents and licenses – much is transmitted by word of mouth from senior to junior. In the last book, Junzō provides a detailed description of the oral lessons he received directly from his seniors over his lifetime. While there is overlap with the lessons formally introduced in the various transmission documents, this section distills what Junzō learned from some of the greatest teachers of Ono-ha Ittō-ryū of his time and reflects his personal thinking on how the various "secrets" of the art are inter-related.

This translation is only of the first book, therefore covers the history of Ono-ha Ittō-ryū from its founding until it was passed to the author, and delves into the details of the personal history of Itō Ittōsai Kagehisa and his immediate successor, Ono Jirōemon Tadaaki. As the author alludes to in the final paragraph of the second chapter, tracing the history of Itō Ittōsai is challenging. First, he was not born into a high-ranking family so there were no contemporaneous accounts of him or his whereabouts either written or retained. Also, the surname *Itō* is common in Japan and there are multiple ways to write it in Japanese script, making tracing his whereabouts as an adult even more challenging. The stories in this book are likely a combination of historical anecdotes found in the resources Junzō collected and what has been handed down within the school as oral history. Of course, this doesn't mean that they are not true, only that there is little verifiable evidence to support their veracity.

The situation of Ono Tadaaki, however, is much less opaque. He was born into a samurai family and eventually served Tokugawa Ieyasu, Japan's first shogun to unify Japan at the end of the Warring States period. His experiences in the service of Ieyasu and Ieyasu's son Hidetada have been documented and subjected to historical inquiry. Likewise for the other figures who had a role in transmitting Ono-ha Ittō-ryū to Tsugaru. Yamaga Sokō is a well-known historical figure in Japan and was considered one of the foremost philosophers of his day, and Obata Kagenori is famous for producing one of Japan's most influential treatises on strategy.

The history of the Tsugaru family is also well-documented[8] and Junzō draws on source material stored by the Tsugaru family in Hirosaki to fully authenticate the history of Ono-ha Ittō-ryū within the Tsugaru Domain.

Though Junzō attempted to provide some clarity on the history of Ittō-ryū using the historical material he could find at the time, the final chapter of its history is not yet written. I hope that scholars continue to explore the origins of this martial art and the people who transmitted it for the benefit of our and future generations. I am humbled and honored to present this translation as part of an effort to bring this history to an English-speaking audience.

Mark Hague
Translator

Endnotes to Translator's Foreword

[1] Sasamori Junzō and Gordon Warner, *This is Kendo: The Art of Japanese Fencing*, (Vermont: Charles E. Tuttle Co. Inc., 1964).

[2] Junzō also wrote *Kendo*, (Tokyo: Obunsha, 1955) and other books.

[3] A naginata is a Japanese halberd.

[4] *Fukuin* (復員)

[5] https://kenshi247.net/blog/2009/08/07/gordon-warner/; downloaded on November 14, 2021.

[6] For more information on the life of Sasamori Takemi, see Sasamori Takemi, *Bushido and Christianity*, trans. Mark Hague (Tokyo: Reigakudo Press, 2016).

[7] *Densho* (伝書)

[8] The Princess Hitachi, wife of retired Emperor Akihito's brother, Prince Masahito, comes from this family.

Secrets of Ittō-ryū

Book One

This book was written in honor of the memories of the founders, Itō Ittōsai Kagehisa, Ono Jirōemon Tadaaki, and the generations of teachers who followed.

Sasamori Junzō

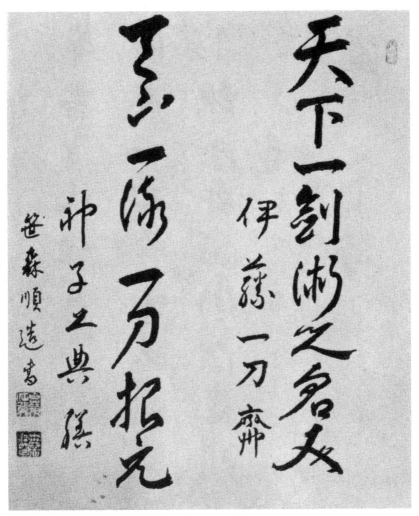

Right: Best swordsman under heaven: Itō Ittōsai.

*Left: Scion of the One-Sword School – the top school in the land:
Mikogami Tenzen.*

Calligraphy by Sasamori Junzō

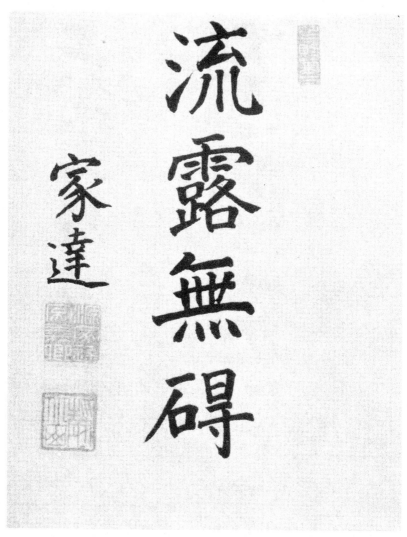

Calligraphy from Tokugawa Iesato passed to the author describing one of the secrets of Ittō-ryū.

Left: calligraphy presented to the author by General Ichinohe Hyōe, Chief Priest of the Meiji Shrine and head of the Gokokukan Dojo.

Right: calligraphy promoting Ittō-ryū by Tsugaru Yasuchika, the 9th Daimyo of the Tsugaru Domain and founder of the domain's educational academy, the Keikokan.

7

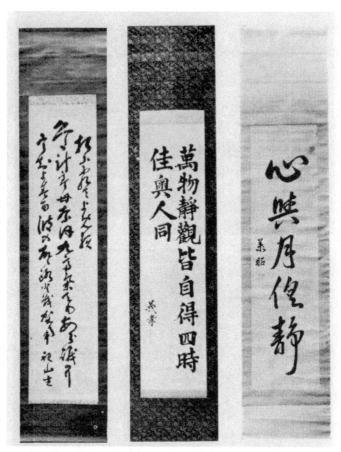

Left: calligraphy from General Asada Nobuoki, head of the Dai Nippon Butokukai and senior adviser to the Gokokukan Dojo.

Middle: calligraphy expressing the concept of "Making all things an ally," one of the secrets of Ittō-ryū, by Tsugaru Yoshitaka, the 14th [and last] generation Tsugaru of his family lineage.

Right: calligraphy expressing the concept of "the Mind and the Moon," one of the secrets of Ittō-ryū, by Tsugaru Tsuguakira, the 11th Daimyo of the Tsugaru Domain.

Wooden statues of Ono Jirōemon Tadaaki and Ono Jirōemon Tadatsune

Demonstration dedicated to the memory of the first two founders of Ono-ha Ittō-ryū in front of their gravestones. On the left is Tsurumi Naritomo Hanshi; on the right is the author.

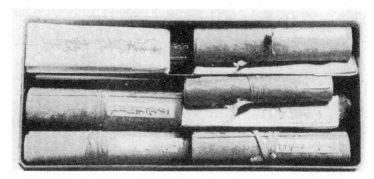

Licenses of Ittō-ryū handed down within the House of Tsugaru.

Demonstration of Ittō-ryū at the Dainanko 600th Anniversary festival at the Minatogawa Shrine. On the left is Takano Sasaburō Hanshi; on the right is the author.

Recent photograph of the author (on his 80th birthday).

FOREWORDS

Foreword by Kimura Tokutarō

Mr. Sasamori Junzō authored the book *Secrets of Ittō-ryū*, providing a full account of the quintessential school of Japanese martial arts. The philosophy, virtues, and principles of this Way of the Sword, which is a legacy of the Japanese people, have been closely guarded secrets handed down by word of mouth since the time of the founder. Through this book, the author scrupulously details the inner mysteries of Ittō-ryū and unflinchingly presents them to the public. This work is a classic of Japanese martial arts that should be required reading for those wishing to master kendo, those pursuing the secret of the ultimate success in life, and those looking for a revered education into the character of the Japanese people.

Kimura Tokutarō
Chairman, All Japan Kendo Federation

Foreword by Saimura Gorō

Ittō-ryū is a famous school of Japanese swordsmanship created by Itō Ittōsai Kagehisa, a man known as the greatest kenjutsu master in the world, and it took the nation by storm in the Edo period. In the mid-Edo period, protective gear and bamboo swords were devised at the Nakanishi Dojo by a student of Ittō-ryū so they could practice applying the techniques of the kumitachi in free play, and this later developed into the training methods of kendo.

So, if you were to learn Ittō-ryū, you would be putting the theory of the sword into actual practice. When you imbue sword theory into actual practice, you win without expecting it, and the older you get, the more these skills are sharpened. This Way of the Sword leads to mastery in all walks of life. Those secrets are provided through this book, which distills over seventy years of hard-earned experience accumulated by Mr. Sasamori Junzō. As one studying the sword myself, I am confident in saying that this is a valuable must-read.

Saimura Gorō
Kendo 10th dan, Hanshi

Foreword by Noda Kō

The founder of Ittō-ryū, Itō Ittōsai, was an unrivaled master swordsman who, through superlative teaching methods, turned out many powerful fighters in later generations. While practicing the kumitachi, he employed both long and short swords in the form of sharpened steel, swords with blunted edges, wooden practice swords, and split bamboo swords covered with cloth.[9] The *onigote*[10] and wooden swords were standard in training, and bamboo training swords could be used without the onigote. But today's kendo method was established and spread after protective gear, the bamboo sword, and free-sparring were devised by Nakanishi Chuzo, a student of Ittō-ryū.

This book, *Secrets of Ittō-ryū*, is a comprehensive work in that it combines the deep understanding of the secrets of Ittō-ryū gained by the author, Mr. Sasamori Junzō, who studied the art for over seventy years starting from early childhood, with instruction on improving one's kendo, which has been gleaned from his many years of experience pouring his heart into teaching kendo at the primary, middle, high school, and college levels.

Noda Kō
Chairman, All Japan Teachers' Kendo Federation

Foreword by Yano Ichirō

These days, the [martial art of] kendo native to our country has spread widely among our young men and has already been adopted into the standardized education curriculum in every school in the country. Steady and proper development is expected in the days ahead. Despite this, the documents of all of our martial traditions, which contain the hidden mysteries that underlie their basic principles, unfortunately, have almost become irretrievably lost today due to them being placed under a doctrine of extreme secrecy.

However, the inner mysteries of the most representative of these schools, Ittō-ryū, reached a pinnacle within the Tsugaru Domain, where it was passed on intact. And Mr. Sasamori Junzō, who was initiated into the legitimate line, opening to the world a clear and detailed description based on his nearly seventy years of study, provides a boundless contribution to Japan's cultural history.

Those who aspire to advance through the world of kendo will come to know well the source of its techniques and principles through this book. My wish is that, after they glimpse the essence of kendo that our ancestors painstakingly created, it will become the guiding principle of their lives.

Yano Ichirō
Chairman, All Japan Business Kendo Federation

15

Foreword by Ishida Kazuto

This book by Mr. Sasamori Junzō, *Secrets of Ittō-ryū*, which I have been eagerly awaiting for many years, has been published. This is truly a great treasure to me, one of his students.

The historical path traced by Itō Ittōsai Kagehisa, the creator of Ittō-ryū, is not entirely clear even to this day, but there is no doubt that he learned his sword techniques from Kanemaki Jisai of the Chūjo-ryū. It is said that after mastering this school he made a warrior pilgrimage throughout the many domains of Japan and engaged in duels with over thirty reputable swordsmen. He mastered the mysteries of the sword, adapted unstoppable sword techniques and distinctive features from various schools, and came up with his own special tactics, all of which led to him eventually creating a first-rate school of his own. This was Ittō-ryū. The story of his visiting Tsurugaoka Hachiman Shrine to pray in the deep of the night and then realizing the miraculous technique of Musōken was a closely held secret of Ittō-ryū that is now widely known.

There are also many legends regarding the second-generation headmaster, Ono Jirōemon Tadaaki. The heroic but tragic tale of how, under the orders of his teacher, he cut down in mortal combat his nefarious fellow-disciple Ono Zenki and was bestowed both the Kamewaritō sword and the secret documents penned by Ittōsai himself, illustrates the gravity with which the transmission of this school was undertaken. Tadaaki served Tokugawa Ieyasu and Hidetada, working as an official instructor to the shogun's family through successive generations. Thus, while working alongside members of the Yagyū Shinkage-ryū, he became a highly respected warrior and received accolades from many feudal lords. Later, Ittō-ryū spawned various factions, such as the Chuya-ha Ittō-ryū, Kaji-ha Ittō-ryū, Nakanishi-ha Ittō-ryū, Hokushin Ittō-ryū, and others, not to mention its importance in

16

laying the groundwork for the [martial art of] kendo that evolved out of the Edo period.

All of the various schools of Japanese swordsmanship, not just Ittō-ryū, had kata that were thought to encompass the school's core doctrine and principles, practiced the techniques within them, had transmission documents that put a premium on instantiating the esoteric secrets of the school through physical mastery, and supplemented these with direct, oral instruction, all of which, of course, eventually led to the unification of the physical techniques with the schools' esoteric principles.[11] But with the advent of the many different types of protective gear and practice swords that proliferated during the middle of the Edo period, together with the insatiable desire to be tested in situations that approximated real fighting, people obsessed too much over winning or losing and started to put a premium on competitive practice with the bamboo swords, and it was not long before the kata that contained the essence of these various schools—not to mention the transmission of their *kumitachi*—gradually became marginalized.

As a result, with a few exceptions, these schools, which had numbered in the hundreds in the past, almost completely died out as the Meiji era gave way to the Taisho and Showa eras. I am truly happy that, despite covering a time period spanning from the Great East Asian War to the emergence of atomic power, Japan's kendo is highly regarded as a path to personal perfection and that competition with bamboo swords flourishes more day-by-day, but it is a terrible shame to see the genesis of this [martial art] disappearing into oblivion, or its essence, which is steeped in such a rich history, teetering on the brink of extinction.

When it comes to Ittō-ryū, however, it should be considered a true miracle that its roots have been preserved intact within the Tsugaru Domain, which is in the northern part of Japan. The main line of transmission of Ittō-ryū started with the second sōke,

17

Tadaaki, passed through the third sōke, Tadatsune, to the fourth sōke, Tadao, and the fifth sōke, Tadakazu, and was then temporarily bestowed upon Tosa-no-Kami Nobuhisa, the Lord of Tsugaru. The extraordinary fact that a feudal lord transmitted the legitimate line himself in this way, and the fact that the capital city of Hirosaki was in a modest and unassuming land far removed from the [political and cultural] center of the country, are considered favorable conditions that brought about this phenomenon. This is nothing other than special providence bestowed upon the martial arts of Japan.

Mr. Sasamori Junzō, from childhood, was taught the legitimate line of Ittō-ryū from the domain instructor, Yamaga Motojiro Takatomo, as handed down by the feudal lords of the Tsugaru Domain and thus is the one who received the techniques of the kumitachi and the school's inner-most secrets in their entirety. This gentleman, who is well-respected as a humble and mild-mannered man of impeccable character and who has developed a broad world-view through his many years of living in America, has already surpassed the age of eighty. It is through this book that he explains in detail the history, techniques, transmission documents, and secrets that he mastered through diligent training over the past seventy years. I would like to give my highest endorsement to this truly authoritative text.

Ishida Kazuto
Chief Justice of the Supreme Court[12]

INTRODUCTION

Ittō-ryū is the epitome of Japanese sword traditions brought to fruition during the Muromachi period by the unparalleled sword master Itō Ittōsai Kagehisa, who passed on lessons of the sword that had been handed down within Japan from antiquity. Moreover, the competitive style of kendo practiced today is something that Ittō-ryū practitioners established during the middle of the Edo period as a way of improving their sword skills. Hence, those who seek to improve in kendo should certainly study Ittō-ryū and draw upon this fount of knowledge.

Whether the Way of the Sword is martial techniques, physical exercise, competitive skills, a philosophy, ethics, or a religion differs depending on one's depth of understanding and mastery of it. The founders who first opened the doors to these ancient schools of fencing reached the deepest mysteries of the sword through religious revelations and lifetimes of training on which they staked life and death. Ittō-ryū didn't just suddenly pop up out of nowhere in the Muromachi period, but it did have a wide-ranging impact. It exemplifies the distinctly Japanese ideology of the sword[13] that originated in, and has been conveyed through, the Japanese people from ancient times, and is the quintessence of Japanese fencing that brought this ideology to a state of perfection.

Examining the historical evidence, there is this passage on the first page of the *Tosenkyo*, a book authored by Ōe no Masafusa, a scholar of ancient Japanese texts:

> The martial virtue[14] existed in the universe from the very beginning, and then, in one instant, cleaved apart Heaven and Earth. This was just like a chick pecking through its egg. The martial eventually became the wellspring of all things and the origin of hundreds of schools of thought.

It is also written in the *Record of Ancient Matters*[15] that the deity Izanagi drew the Ten-Fist-Saber[16] hanging at his side and cut off the head of his son, Kagutsuchi, before giving birth to sixteen new gods who founded Japan.[17] Around this time there was also the deity Takemikazuchi, who was later worshiped as a martial god. Later, when the deity Amaterasu-Ōmikami received the Ten-Fist-Saber from the deity Susanoo and snapped it into three pieces, she gave birth to three more gods.[18] Due to these legends, our ancestors came to be viewed as always wielding a sword to do good deeds or propagate new life. When Susanoo hacked off the middle tail of the eight-headed dragon Yamata no Orochi, sliced it open, and looked inside, he discovered the sword called the *Tsumugari-no-Tachi*.[19] Later, this sword would be referred to as the *Grass-mowing Sword*.[20] And the sword that hung by the side of the deity Onamuchi was called the *Ikutachi*,[21] which means *living sword* and *sword that confers long life*. After that, the legend emerged of Takemikazuchi using the Ten-Fist-Saber in the Izumo Domain's Fifty Lands of Obama.

In the ancient past, swords of Japan were called *tsurugi* or *tsumugari*, and written with the character 剣. This has the meaning of *cleanly severing* and *piercing into*. The Japanese people, from time immemorial, have also called the sword *tachi*, which can be written with the characters, 太刀, meaning *large blade*, or these, 多知, meaning *great wisdom*. They have come to view the sword as cleaving one into two, two into four, and adding to and multiplying that number, and then integrating everything back into one. This describes a process of first creating, further developing, and finally bringing to perfection, and this is how sword techniques develop.

It is said of the martial arts of Japan that "The martial arts of the gods do not kill."[22] This, however, doesn't just mean that the martial arts are not for killing. The character for martial, 武, can be read as *bu* and also *mu*, which is a homonym for, 産,[23] that contains the meaning of *bringing forth, producing*, and *connecting*. Our ancestors considered the origin of life and the work of creation as coming through the sword and the spear, and these became profound spiritual instruments that came to symbolize the creation of the Japanese people. It is also said that arms, written as, 兵 (*hei*), led to peace, written as, 平 (*hei*), so the *techniques of wielding arms, heijutsu* (兵術), came to be called the *techniques of peace, heijutsu* (平術). At the micro level they came to teach these as the skills of harmonizing with other people and, at a broader level, as the skills of bringing peace to the world. The moral principles derived from the distinctive characteristics of this creation and peaceful existence begat various kinds of virtuous behavior applied in daily life such as: growth and edification; benevolence and mercy; magnanimity and generosity; justice and courage; truth [24] and righteousness; cleanliness and purity; courtesy and respect; simplicity and elegance; fairness and justness; service and sacrifice; cooperation and mutual assistance; diligence and hard work; and improvement and progress. No matter the era, the fundamental essence of the Way of the Sword has come to be taught as being built upon this enduring moral and philosophical foundation, both at the individual and societal levels.

Other countries' views of the martial are completely different. The historical commentary that explains the etymology of the Chinese character for *martial* has this to say:

> According to King Zhuang of Chu:[25] In the written script, the stopping of weapons constitutes the martial. Now in the case of the martial, it means prohibiting violence, collecting weapons, preserving the great, establishing merit, bringing peace to the people, uniting the masses, and making resources abundant.[26]

The ancient Chinese considered armaments to be instruments of evil, so they defined the character for martial, i.e., *bu* (武), to mean *stopping them*. Thus, Lao-tzu said:

> Fine weapons are instruments of evil. They are hated by men.[27]

And through verses like the following, this same individual seemed to believe that the ultimate purpose of a sword was something harmful that needed to be kept in check:

> Weapons are instruments of evil, not the instruments of a good ruler. When he uses them unavoidably, he regards calm restraint as the best principle.[28]

So the negative view in other countries of swords as evil weapons and the positive view of them in Japan as items to treasure are as different as night and day.

Historically, the development of Japanese swordsmanship went hand-in-hand with changes in Japanese society. The Way of the Sword in Japan that originated in antiquity suddenly gained prominence in the Warring States period. Over a span of several hundred years, hardened warriors maneuvered around battlefields mounted on horseback or on foot and initiated skirmishes by launching arrows from a long distance. Then they moved forward and mowed down their opponents with halberds or sliced through them with spears, and after they came into close contact, drew their swords to cut them down. When their swords broke, they would grapple, throwing their opponents to the ground and finishing them off with their daggers.[29] Multitudes of warriors fought it out on the battlefield using all types of weapons in an integrated fashion under the headings of different military disciplines. These disciplines were common knowledge among military men of the time, who referred to them as the *Eighteen Basic Military Arts* or the *Fourteen Basic Military Arts*.

These warriors frequently faced life and death situations, and they forged courageous spirits and polished their martial skills on actual battlefields where they devised all kinds of ingenious ways to defeat their enemies. They defended their domains, lived out their lives, and in the end, mastered their own minds, never wavering in the face of life or death, fostering their moral character, and learning to live in times of both war and peace. They never lost sight of the compassion of honoring the souls of worthy opponents who fell under their blades. They took the know-how, experience, technical skills, and maxims developed on the battlefield and created new methods of combat. They opened schools founded upon the principles of the pre-eminent laws of Heaven and Earth and the teachings of the sages, and took on students who then handed down these lessons to their descendants. After this assortment of schools, branches, and factions of distinctly Japanese martial arts came into existence,

23

they shone brilliantly. Above all, the superior among these, which was passed on to future generations and founded upon the bedrock of ingenuity and prosperity, pursuit of spiritual peace, and unparalleled strength, was Ittō-ryū, founded by Itō Ittōsai Kagehisa. From the Muromachi through the Edo periods, shoguns, daimyo, and many powerful warriors hailed from this school.

The Meiji Restoration was a time when all kinds of reforms accompanied the abolition of Japan's feudal system and, due to the prohibition against wearing swords, the old-style military arts fell into a brief decline. The might of the atom bomb seen during World War II rendered conventional weapons ineffective. In this day and age there isn't a madman alive who would stand up against a ballistic missile or hydrogen bomb while wielding a sword. That notwithstanding, the moral precepts, philosophies, mental skills, and physical techniques developed in these schools and brought to fruition by the painstaking efforts, experiences, ingenuity, training, hard-earned knowledge, and enlightenment of the founders of these schools and factions of martial traditions that had been passed down among the people of Japan for such a long time, and their tempering by successive generations of masters, not to mention the privations experienced by their students, are of enduring value as Japan's historical legacy. They have become highly regarded standards of athletic competition that nurture the mind and body, and have become guiding tenets of life recast for a new era. They should be preserved, promoted, and made available to the public in perpetuity.

It is truly regrettable that not long after a few major shocks in Japan's history the secret transmission documents that had once been considered priceless family treasures were buried away and forgotten. That so many of these ancient artifacts disappeared into thin air within such a short period of time was because our ancestors placed such a premium on the secrets of their schools that they kept them under lock and key as their exclusive

24

possessions and nearly all those who would have been devoted to passing them on died off.

Our forebears forbade their children and students from writing anything down, forcing them instead to learn these lessons by etching them into their minds and muscle memory through oral instruction. Moreover, it was impermissible to show or divulge the contents of the transmission scrolls to others, and the most secret of their lessons were jealously guarded and passed on to only one person in a patrilineal succession, which made it difficult to convey, circulate, promulgate, preserve, promote, or develop these priceless teachings. So, it is a real shame that, these days, those who could do the actual techniques have all passed away and many of the old scrolls containing these secrets that were stored in the bowels of prestigious samurai households only have their titles on them, don't describe the sequence of techniques within, or the origins of the names of the techniques, or provide a clue as to how to perform them. As a consequence, the research into, investigation of, and transmission to future generations of the tenets of these schools, branches, and factions of martial arts are urgently needed today in order to preserve the cultural history of the Japanese people.

Starting in the 1890s, from the age of seven or eight, I learned the fundamental basics of Ittō-ryū at the Hokushindo Dojo in Hirosaki City from Tsushima Kenpachi, the official kenjutsu instructor of the former Tsugaru Domain. I kept up my training throughout middle and high school, learning Ittō-ryū from the sword master Nakahata Hidegoro, continuing to study under him until he passed away at the advanced age of eighty-two. Also, Yamaga Sokō's [30] fourth generation descendent, Yamaga Hachirozaemon Takami, received the full transmission of the secrets of Ittō-ryū from Ono Jirōemon Tadayoshi, the Yamaga family having served the Tsugaru Domain over successive generations as teachers of both military strategy and the martial art of Ittō-ryū. Takami's great-great grandson, Takatomo, passed to me all of the secret transmission scrolls of Ittō-ryū handed down within the Yamaga family as well as Takami's wooden practice sword that was fashioned in 1770. I was also provided full and direct initiation into the main line of Ittō-ryū that was passed down through the House of Tsugaru, which maintained the legitimate line of the school ever since Ono Jirōemon Tadakazu bequeathed it to Tsugaru Tosa-no-kami Nobuhisa, and inherited all of the techniques of Ittō-ryū, the transmission scrolls, the recorded oral traditions, and other material explaining the secrets of the school. I teamed up with other like-minded individuals, such as Ichikawa Umon and Shibuya Fumio, to establish the Gokokukan Dojo in Hirosaki City and promoted many different types of ancient martial arts there, with a particular emphasis on the research of Ittō-ryū.

In 1930, on the occasion of the tenth anniversary of the Enshrinement Ceremony at Meiji Shrine, [31] those who were preserving the various schools, branches, and factions of martial arts from all over Japan came together under the auspices of the Ministry of Home Affairs, and with Ichinohe Hyōe as the Chairman, put on a major demonstration dedicated to the preservation of Japanese martial arts.[32] During this demonstration, priceless and consummate skills—the product of a thousand-year effort to diligently pass them down from our ancestors—could be glimpsed, even if hazily, and garnered great interest. The arts selected to demonstrate at the Hibiya Municipal Hall on that day were kendo, judo, spear fighting, sword drawing, halberd, short staff, long staff, sickle and chain, bayonet, karate, grappling in armor,[33] arresting techniques, and archery; and outside the hall, equestrian techniques and military swimming—fifteen types in all. From among the hundreds of prestigious schools in Japan, there were twenty-five kenjutsu traditions selected to demonstrate. Listing them in order of appearance, they were: Ōishi Shinkage-ryū, Tenshin Shoden Katori Shinto-ryū, Suifu-ryū, Shinkage-ryū, Hokushin Ittō-ryū, Mugai-ryū, Shinto Munen-ryū, Keishi-ryū, Kōshi Gogyō no Kata, Tenshin-ryū, Ono-ha Ittō-ryū, Greater Japan Imperial Kendo Kata, Ittō Shōden Mutō-ryū, Jikishinkage-ryū, Toda-ryū, Chuwa Ittō-ryū, Kaishin-ryū, Rikishin-ryū, Kurama-ryū, Bokuden-ryū, Unkō-ryū, Tennen Rishin-ryū, Tamiya-ryū, Yamaguchi Ittō-ryū, and Maniwa Nen-ryū. The prestigious schools listed above were specially selected to be reviewed by the Imperial Family. Ono-ha Ittō-ryū shared that honor, and I demonstrated the secret Habiki kata with Takasugi Kenkichi.

On November 3, 1933, at the Meiji Jingu Athletic Convention held at the Nippon Seinenkan, I demonstrated Ittō-ryū's Odachi kata with Takano Sasaburō. I demonstrated with him again in 1935 at the Dainanko 600th Anniversary festival at the Minatogawa Shrine,[34] where we exhibited Ono-ha Ittō-ryū's many techniques. On March 18, 1936, the twelve main schools that hailed from the two southern domains of Tsugaru held a demonstration of traditional martial arts at the Too Gijuku [Junior-Senior High School] in Hirosaki City to welcome both Prince Chichibu-no-Miya and his wife.[35] These were: Kaji-ha Ittō-ryū, Ono-ha Ittō-ryū, Toda-ryū, Bokuden-ryū, Shinmusō Hayashizaki-ryū, Anazawa-ryū, Chokugen-ryū, Yagyu-ryū, Kusaka Shin-ryū (日下真流), Kusaka Shin-ryū (日下新流), Ito-ryū (一当流), and the Hongaku Kokki-ryū. I demonstrated Ono-ha Ittō-ryū's Habiki kata with Tsurumi Naritomo, the Hosshatō kata with Kodate Toshio, the Goten kata with Fujiwara Shintaro, and moreover, presented the secret transmission scrolls[36] of Ono-ha Ittō-ryū for imperial review.

After I transferred to Tokyo in November 1939, I had many opportunities to publicly demonstrate the techniques of Ono-ha Ittō-ryū at all kinds of martial arts exhibitions and conventions. On October 15, 1964, I performed Ittō-ryū's Goten kata with Tsurumi Naritomo at the Tokyo martial arts exhibition held at the refurbished Nippon Budokan to celebrate the games of the XVIII Olympiad.[37] I also established the Reigakudō Dojo in my personal residence and offered it for the benefit of those who were enthusiastic about practicing Ittō-ryū and other martial arts.

Starting from a young age and spanning a period of over seventy years, I devoted myself to the school of Ittō-ryū that was passed on from the ancients, and the more I investigated its principles, the deeper I got into them, and the more I pursued the Way, the more the path just seemed to go further and further. Nakanishi Chūbe (Chusuke) Tsugusmasa,[38] the fourth-generation Nakanishi who studied under Ono Jirōemon Tadakazu, wrote the following *waka* poem in his own hand on his self-portrait:

尋ねても

Though you seek,

またたづねても

And though you seek again,

たづねても

And though you seek,

たづねあたらぬ

You seek in vain

剣術の道

The Way of Kenjutsu

The scroll this was written on was presented to Sudō Hanbei, Tsugumasa's student, and was passed to me from the Sudō family later. The heart of the poem conveys well the subtle profundity of the Way of the Sword. Seeking out, exhaustively studying, and then demonstrating the wisdom and superhuman skills of the masters going back to the founder was virtually impossible, but I wracked my brain to comprehend and master the true secrets and techniques of Ittō-ryū that have been conveyed directly from the founder from generation to generation, collected and compiled background material containing the actual meaning of the lessons and physical techniques, classified them, catalogued them, and arranged them in order, trying to fully ensure the accuracy of their explanations. After spending seventy years focusing on this and after many drafts, I was finally able to finish a manuscript and publish it as this book.

Since ancient times there has been a code that before entering a traditional school of martial arts to study, one swears a blood oath that he will keep its lessons strictly secret and accept the consequences of divine retribution if he were to divulge or show these most private teachings to outsiders. But the reason I took it upon myself to make these lessons open to the public now was to pass these extraordinary principles and profound techniques on to future generations of those studying the sword, publicly honor the service to society our ancestors took so much trouble to render, and to preserve, convey, and promote the artistic and spiritual culture unique to our magnificent country. Elucidating the essential mysteries of Ittō-ryū is of tremendous value to those studying kendo, which was derived from Ittō-ryū. And it is my hope that this public disclosure will produce many devotees who are interested in learning authentic ancient martial arts getting together with other like-minded individuals to further their research, and that the lessons they glean from them will turn into guiding principles for a new generation of kendoka and will become a fountainhead of mental and physical cultivation. Moreover, if it were to comprise material that provided a glimpse into the unique thinking and extraordinary behavior of Japan to those who have never even held a sword, I would be extremely delighted.

Sasamori Junzō
May 18, 1965
On the occasion of my 80th birthday

Endnotes to Forewords

[9] *Fukuro shinai* (袋竹刀)

[10] Oversized protective gloves unique to Ittō-ryū.

[11] *Jiri itchi* (事理一致)

[12] Aside from being Japan's fifth Chief Justice of the Supreme Court from 1969 to 1973, Ishida Kazuto was the fifth sōke of Ittō Shoden Muto-ryū, the branch of Ittō-ryū created by Yamaoka Tesshū. Born in Fukui Prefecture in 1903, Ishida also practiced kendo and held memberships in the Yagyūkai and the All-Japan Kendo Federation. He died on May 9, 1979.

[13] *Tsurugi-tachi no shisō* (剣太刀の思想)

[14] *Bu* (武)

[15] Ō no Yasumaru, *Record of Ancient Matters* (*Kojiki*), an early chronicle of Japanese myths thought to have been written circa 711-712 AD.

[16] *Totsuka-no-Tsurugi* (十拳剣)

[17] 十六柱の命

[18] These were the Three Goddesses of Munakata.

[19] This sword, along with a mirror and jewels, became one of Japan's Three Imperial Regalia.

[20] *Kusanagi-no-Tachi* (草薙の剣)

[21] 生太刀

[22] *Jinbu Fusatsu* (神撫不殺). Phrase attributed to King Wen of Zhou (1152-1056).

[23] This character can also be read as *umu* and *musubu*.

[24] *Shinei* (真鋭)

[25] King Zhuang (楚荘王) was a monarch of the Zhou dynasty who reigned from 613-591 B.C. during the Spring and Autumn period in ancient China.

[26] See Robin McNeal's *Conquer and Govern: Early Chinese Military Texts from the Yizhou Shu*, (Honolulu: University of Hawaii Press, 2012) pp. 48-49.

[27] Original Chinese reads: 夫佳兵者不祥之器　物或悪之. Lao Tzu, *Tao Te Ching*, in Chapter 31, *A Source Book in Chinese Philosophy*, trans. and ed. Wing-Tsit Chan (Princeton: Princeton University Press) p. 155.

[28] Ibid.

[29] *Yoroidōshi* (鎧通し)

[30] Yamaga Sokō (1622-1685) was a neo-Confucian scholar, philosopher, and strategist who initially worked for the Tokugawa Bakufu. His works helped define the role of the samurai within the peaceful Tokugawa era. He was eventually exiled to the Akō domain by Hoshina Masayuki after breaking from Tokugawa orthodoxy. He also studied Ittō-ryū under Obata Kagenori.

[31] *Chinzakinensai* (November 1): The souls of Emperor Meiji and Empress Shoken were enshrined at Meiji Jingu on November 1, 1920. This ceremony celebrates the anniversary of this enshrinement.

[32] *Nihon Budō Kata Hōnō Enbu Taikai* (日本武道形奉納演武大会).

[33] *Jingu jutsu* (陣具術).

[34] Festival celebrating the 600th anniversary of the death of Kusunoki Masashige.

[35] Junzō would have been the Chancellor of the Too Gijuku at this time.

[36] *Densho* (伝書).

[37] These were the 1964 Summer Olympics held in Tokyo, the first time the Olympics were held in Asia.

[38] 中西忠兵衛子正

CHAPTER ONE

Lineage of Ono-ha Ittō-ryū

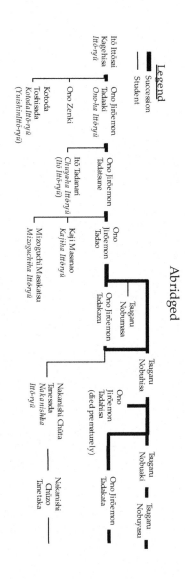

Abridged

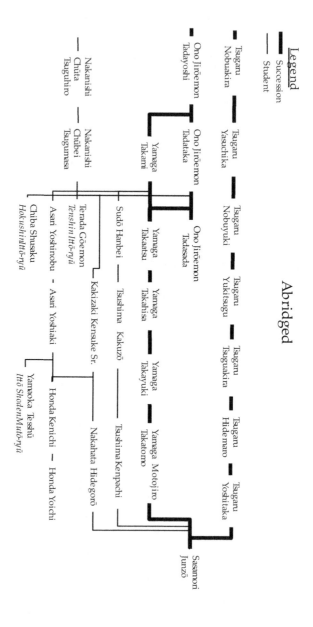

CHAPTER TWO

Life of Itō Ittōsai Kagehisa: Founder of Ittō-ryū

The Birth of Ittō-ryū

Ittō-ryū is an acclaimed martial art of the day rooted in the history of Japan. To provide a brief narrative of this past, following Prince Yamato Takeru-no-Mikoto, who established the three profound aspects of swordsmanship[39] of Heaven, Earth, and Man, which was part of the founding myths of ancient Japan, the sword master Kuninazu-no-Mahito created the divinely inspired *Ichi-no-Tachi* style of swordsmanship. Emperor Kammu built the Hall of Martial Virtue [40] where he viewed martial arts training and demonstrations. Hachiman Taro Yoshiie[41] added Yin and Yang to the three aspects of Heaven, Earth, and Man, creating a total of five profound aspects.[42]

Thereafter, Chūjō Hyogonosuke Nagahide emerged from the gates of legendary sword master Nen Ami Jion's school of Nen-ryū, and Ōhashi Kageyuzaemon, after learning Chūjō-ryū, passed on this tradition to Toda Kurōemon Nagaie. Toda's descendants, Toda Kurōemon Kageie and Toda Kagemasa, became famous fencing masters. Kanemaki Jisai, a top student of the Todas, created Kanemaki-ryū, which became famous for its secret Supreme Adamant[43] Goten kata.

But the one who stands head and shoulders above the rest throughout this entire history for eclipsing his own master is Itō Ittōsai Kagehisa. Ittōsai, upon experiencing a religious revelation[44] and deeply contemplating the mysteries of sword techniques that he innovated and mastered through his unbeatable skills forged in the fire of a host of deadly bouts, established the broad curriculum of Ittō-ryū. After its creation, it evolved into something that reflected brilliantly upon the Japanese martial arts by ushering in epoch-making historical developments in both the cultural and martial traditions of Japan. And it was in the Muromachi period that it blazed new trails in these areas.

Birth and Early Childhood

Itō Ittōsai Kagehisa was born on August 5, 1550,[*] on the island of Ōshima, which lies off the coast of the Izu peninsula, as the son of Itō Yaemon Tomoie, a descendant of Itō Nyudō Kagechika. He was given the name Maehara Yagoro at birth. He had a brawny build as a child, was stronger than others, yet agile, and from a young age he liked to entertain himself by jumping and running. He was naturally fierce, and when viewed from afar while roughhousing with his mates, it looked as if a ferocious eagle flew amongst a cluster of chickens, making them scatter. He took up fishing at the age of eight. He would haul a small boat into the sea and frolic among the surging waves, surprising his neighbors with the large fish he hauled up by hand. As he grew older, he cut a striking image, with his muscular physique, piercing gaze,

---

[*] There is an alternate theory that he was born in Shikoku. There is also another theory that he was born on August 5, 1561 (the third year of Eiroku 永禄).

bronze-colored skin, and hair hanging down around his shoulders. He constantly trained himself physically and mentally by diving into the waves of the raging sea facing Mt. Mihara, which was spitting fire day and night, and though he was forging a bold and courageous spirit, his neighbors feared him and called him a demon. But his pure and innocent nature was such that he genuinely hated injustice and enjoyed helping those who were weaker. Though in his youth he passed the time on Ōshima Island, the land of his birth, it was not where he wanted to live for the rest of his life. So, he looked to the western sky, thinking that there must be a way to get to the mainland, and made up his mind to get away from his ancestral home.

From Ōshima to Izu
First Duel with Ippō

When it finally came time to leave the island of his birth, Yagoro grabbed a plank of wood under his arm and plunged into the sea all by himself. He swam to nearby Izu and made his way to Mishima Village, where he took up residence in the Mishima Shrine doing odd jobs for the elders there. The villagers were frightened by his appearance, clamoring that an island goblin had come ashore, and none dared get close.

Around that time a swordsman named Toda Ippō, a student of Toda Echigo-no-Kami Shigemasa, arrived and lorded his military exploits over the villagers. Hearing this and wanting to test his own skills against Ippō, Yagoro challenged him to a match.

Ippō, who was well-known as a distinguished sword teacher, rode into town in grand style attended by dozens of his students. Yagoro wandered out alone to size him up, and then met Oribe, the head of the shrine, to receive his blessing. Once Yagoro and Ippō finished their personal preparations, they faced each other in the garden in front of the shrine. Ippō boasted of his previous exploits and took pride in his own splendid attire while looking down his nose at the shabbily dressed Yagoro. He became preoccupied with impressing the crowd, only thinking about striking flashy poses, so his distance was off and he wasn't at all prepared. Yagoro, on the other hand, intently concentrated on his opponent, got the measure of him, and then sprang forward like a bird in flight without bothering to touch sword tips. He took Ippō completely by surprise, hitting him hard on the shoulder and cutting down to his waist, knocking him unconscious where he stood. Ippō was humiliated and left Mishima in disgrace. At the time, Yagoro was barely fourteen years old.

Receiving the Urn-splitting Sword

Oribe rewarded Yagoro's courage by presenting him with the Mishima Shrine's treasured *Ichimonji* sword, saying: "The master swordsmith, Ichimonji, from ancient Bizen, pursuing a long-cherished dream, shut himself up in this shrine for thirty-seven days, devoted himself to the forging process, and pounded his heart and soul into this blade. After he finished, he presented it to the shrine. The naked blade had been wrapped in a straw rope and hung from the rafters, edge down, for many years until, one day, it suddenly cut through the rope and dropped onto a sake urn that had been placed as an offering on an altar below, cutting it cleanly in two. Something this sharp has no equal in the world. We now ask at this altar that you take it." Yagoro was delighted and graciously accepted. Thereafter, he became an honored guest of Oribe.

One night a short time later, dozens of brigands streamed into the grounds of Oribe's mansion and attacked. They were, perhaps, people incited by Ippō or survivors of a defeated neighboring domain seeking revenge. Yagoro sprang into action and easily cut down seven of the thugs on the spot before the rest, upon seeing this, scattered in all directions. One of the fleeing bandits lost his way, hid behind an earthenware sake urn, and ran around it to escape when he was spotted by Yagoro. Seeing him trying to get away, Yagoro brought his sword down and cut both the ruffian and the urn completely in two. After this incident, he named this sword the *Urn-splitting Sword* (*Kamewari no katana* 甕割の刀) and it became a treasure of Ittō-ryū passed down from generation to generation of headmasters ever since. It's rumored to have been dedicated to the Nikko Shrine and stored there in a mausoleum.[†]

Mastering the Kanemaki-ryū and Hankan-ryū

Maehara Yagoro's determination to learn martial arts grew ever stronger and he left Mishima for the east to visit famous martial arts masters there. At the time, the techniques of the Supreme Adamant Sword[45] were considered the highest-level secrets of swordsmanship, and he traveled to Edo to visit the renowned expert of Chujō-ryū, Kanemaki Jisai Michiie. From Jisai he learned the short sword of Chujō-ryū and the techniques of the mid-length sword,[46] which were special tactics devised by Jisai. Because Yagoro diligently practiced day and night with single-minded devotion, within a few years he became so good that none of his fellow students could match him. He attained such confidence in himself that he approached Jisai:

"I have mastered the secrets of your curriculum, so I ask that you release me from your school," he asked.

[†] Even though it has been searched for, the whereabouts of the Kamewaritō are unknown as of this writing.

Jisai refused his request saying, "You haven't yet completed all of my instruction; it hasn't even been five years since you started. How are you able to understand the mysteries of our school?"

"If you, teacher, doubt my word, would you test me just once?" Yagoro replied.

With that, Jisai picked up a wooden practice sword[47] and faced Yagoro – three times he faced him and three times he was unable to defeat him. Jisai was astonished at Yagoro's progress and prowess, and when he asked how he was able to attain such a high level of mastery so quickly, Yagoro replied:

"When you, teacher, go to strike me, what you are about to do is reflected in my mind. I just react to it. It's just like when you have an itch on your head and your hand just naturally goes there to scratch. This phenomenon is a marvel of the mind and not something I was taught by you."

Jisai was deeply impressed by this and bestowed upon Yagoro the secrets of his school and the *Myōken*, *Zetsumyōken*, *Shinken*, *Kinshichō Ōken*, and *Dokumyōken* techniques which comprise the kata of Goten, the highest-level teachings of Jisai's school. Yagoro was pleased, thanked Jisai for all he had done for him, and departed. Yagoro's reputation as a student who eclipsed his own teacher grew and he eventually became much more famous than Jisai, earning the reputation as the finest swordsman in all of the land. But, although he far exceeded his master, he still held a deep debt of gratitude toward him, and later, after he created Ittō-ryū and developed the many marvelous techniques within it, he honored Jisai by elevating the sword techniques of Goten that he learned from him to the highest-level secrets of Ittō-ryū. On the one hand, Ittōsai was bold and brash, but on the other, he had the purity of intentions of someone who deeply revered his former master. After departing with Jisai's blessing, Yagoro visited other schools, studied the Hankan-ryū[48] of Minamoto Itō, and left after mastering its secrets in short order.

Yagoro set out on a journey to tour the various provinces of Japan. It was a time when the power and authority of the Ashikaga Shogunate had suddenly declined, rivals emerged in the surrounding domains, the country was plunged into civil war, and social turmoil was the order of the day. Yagoro faced this situation squarely, took it as an opportunity to train his mind and body and foster a warrior spirit, proceeded alone, confronted danger, escaped the jaws of death, and forged personal courage and martial skill. He traveled to all the different domains, and whether threading his way through throngs of people in city streets, stretching out in the grassy plains, or sleeping deep in the mountains, he viewed the sun and the moon, the stars in heaven, the clouds in the sky, and the animals and plants in the forest as his teachers. And when he visited the most renowned sword masters of the day and fought it out with them to decide who was the best, he left it up to them to choose whether they wanted to use sharpened steel blades,[49] the wooden practice sword, or something else. He saw through everything they threw at him and always beat them, though, not losing a single match. He always went easy on those who lost, however, and never took their lives needlessly. And if any of them asked, he would gladly accept them as students and teach them.

Founding of Ittō-ryū

Maehara Yagoro changed his name to Itō Yagoro Kagehisa, crisscrossed the many domains of Japan, met a number of skilled opponents and defeated them all, researched other schools, honed his own skills, and gained more and more confidence in his own abilities. Despite this, he still wasn't able to find true peace of mind. So one year, resolving that he needed to do more to further nurture his spirit, he entered a Buddhist temple in the middle of winter, quietly sat by himself while gripping a steel *nyoi*,[50] calmed his mind, and focused on meditation. But no matter how much he tried, in the beginning, idle thoughts crowded his mind, and no matter how hard he tried to chase them away, fantastical images billowed up out of nowhere like clouds. He was unable to unify his spirit. He realized this was due to his own inflated ego and that he was being swayed by outside forces, so he redoubled his efforts, fasted, and turned this over in his mind. After several days of focusing intensely, he slid into a perfect state of deep spiritual reverie and before he knew it the steel nyoi in his palms strangely started to feel hot, like he was holding a flame. *What's happening!* he thought, and when his attention shifted, this time the nyoi froze and it felt like he was holding on to ice.

Kagehisa was deeply affected by this bizarre phenomenon, wracked his brain to find the underlying principles behind it, and finally realized that the changes between hot and cold within the steel nyoi came from the circulation of his own vital energy,[51] which flowed out of his hands and into the steel nyoi and then reversed direction and conveyed the heat and cold back to himself, and it was this that he sensed. After a long period of intense practice nurturing this skill, he reached the point where he was able to consciously direct the flow of this vital energy into the steel nyoi in his hands at will. Through this extraordinary experience, he came to realize the mind directs the body and the body directs the sword, so the mind, sword, and body are as one. He named this profound principle of the sword and the mind being as one[52] the *One-Mind-Sword*.[53] He saw the *One Mind* as bringing all things physical under the control of the mind, learned how to use this to respond flawlessly to whatever his opponent threw at him, and obtained the profound principle of using the mind, body, and sword combined as a single entity.[54] He came up with a name for what he discovered and called it *Ittō-ryū*,[55] and took the name *Ittōsai* for himself.

Best Swordsman Under Heaven

Itō Ittōsai Kagehisa never put down roots but swaggered about Japan as if he owned it. He traveled to castle towns and other bustling areas of the country where he stayed at inns, hanging out a sign-board that read: *Itō Ittōsai Kagehisa, The Best Swordsman Under Heaven*. This wasn't because he had an arrogant attitude, nor was it due to him trying to be provocative. On the contrary, it was to guard against becoming arrogant, reflected his desire to seek continuous improvement with humility, was a search for a worthy teacher, and was a fearless challenge to any skilled opponents who may have been hiding nearby. Because he would hang the sign outside the inn for five, ten, thirty, and even fifty days, people would find out he was there and challenge him to a duel. Not one of his challengers ever beat him, though, and many ended up learning swordsmanship from him as his student.

If Ittōsai were to hear of a famous warrior, he would happily travel hundreds of miles to meet him and test his skills. When word reached others of Ittōsai's feats of arms, those who wanted to fight him would travel from afar, and Ittōsai would always graciously greet them and accept their challenge. But in the end, none ever bested him. Ittōsai's unique skills with the sword slowly but surely became more refined, he matured emotionally, lived up to the reputation as the best swordsman in the land, and the glory of his fighting exploits spread far and wide. The number of those who wanted to study under him steadily grew. He took on students; however, having no desire for fame nor caring to kowtow to royalty or receive a stipend by serving a feudal lord, he was never concerned with worldly affairs [56] and enjoyed the carefree life of a loner, finding boundless delight in the creation and refinement of the inner secrets of Ittō-ryū.

The Story of Hosshatō

When Ittōsai was in Kyoto,[‡] a man challenged him to a duel. Ittōsai accepted and beat the challenger on the spot. While asking to be accepted as his student, this man came up with a devious scheme to increase his own reputation within the capital by killing Ittōsai, who was far better. Under the pretext of becoming students, he, along with some other co-conspirators, joined Ittōsai's school while looking for the right time to strike. They all knew that, no matter how many in number, they would have no hope of success if they attacked Ittōsai in the open, so they devised a secret and cowardly plan to take him by surprise. They learned from a previous acquaintance that when Ittōsai visited Kyoto he would sometimes enjoy the company of a local woman. The plotters cozied up to her and won her over with cash and other gifts. They then fooled her into joining their plot and used her to invite Ittōsai to dinner one night where she wined and dined him by plying him with rice wine and serving him tea and roasted soybeans. While merrily enjoying himself, he let his guard down and became dead drunk. As any good hostess would, the woman spread out bedding in the middle of the room and laid him down to sleep. She was someone he normally trusted, so Ittōsai, feeling drunk and not considering the consequences, fell into a deep sleep.

It was in the middle of summer and the woman hung a mosquito net over him to keep him comfortable. After making sure he was sound asleep, she quietly removed his long and short swords from near his pillow and hid them. As previously arranged, a little after midnight she guided the gang of more than a dozen goons to Ittōsai's room from a nearby room where they

---

[‡] There is an alternate theory that this happened in Kamakura. There are also those who believe this story was fabricated.

had been hiding. From there they burst into his room through an unlocked door. First, they cut the strings on the four corners of Ittōsai's mosquito net, dropping it onto him, and then started slashing from all sides. Ittōsai, sensing impending danger, opened his eyes in the nick of time and searched around his pillow, but his two swords were gone. He jumped back, out from under a blade slicing down toward him, and darted back and forth under the net to avoid the blows streaking down like thunderbolts. He eventually managed to squirm his way out from under the netting. Grabbing whatever bowls and sake cups left over from dinner he could get his hands on, he hurled them at his attackers in rapid fire. When one of his assailants flinched, Ittōsai dove at him, grabbed his sword, and wrenched it from his grip. Ittōsai, who had just been jarred awaked from a deep sleep and remained unscathed despite being caught off-guard without any weapons, fought like a man possessed after he got a sword. With the fury of a raging lion, he cut, stabbed, and slashed, and before he knew it, he was dealing deep cuts and mortal wounds to his assailants. When those who were unscathed saw their friends dropping like flies under his blade, they scattered in terror. Ittōsai survived the assault without even a minor scratch.

Ittōsai considered the sword techniques of Hosshatō[57] he used that night as deep secrets of Ittō-ryū that he highly valued for saving his life, and he taught these to later generations of students. Moreover, he thought to himself that it was unacceptable for a warrior to lower his guard and thoughtlessly invite his own defeat by letting himself get carried away by youthful impetuousness or wallowing in sensual pleasure. After this incident, he honed the sword of Hossha as a mystical guide for life that cut away arrogance and carnal desires within himself and that cut down treacherous conspiracies launched against him by the outside world. He left the following lessons for future generations:

1: Keep out of range of your opponents' attack and see what they are up to.

2: Grab whatever you can get your hands on and randomly hurl them at your attackers to make them flinch.

3: Charge your enemy and take away whatever sharp-edged weapons they have and use them for yourself.

4: Use the tried-and-true method of winning by boldly crossing into the zone of death under your opponents' blade to get in close, stick with them so they can't get away, and then stab and slash into their vulnerable points.

5: Take a bird's eye view of your opponents, render the final judgement of Hossha from an all-encompassing perspective, and completely dominate them.

The ultimate lesson of Hossha is that it teaches one to remain safe by ridding oneself of threats to his life that demand the use of it in the first place.

The man, Ittōsai, who possessed an exceedingly rare and powerful physique and had no shortage of fighting spirit, got carried away by hot-blooded desires, and when he lost himself in a night of revelry, he dropped his guard, opened himself up to attack, and it was there where danger snuck up on him. Had he been just an ordinary man it probably would have been the end of him. But, as one might expect, because he was massively built and combined unusually quick reflexes, grit, and superb skill, he seamlessly responded to whatever his opponents threw at him, and slashed, cut, and stabbed his way through the gang of thugs who conspired against him, snatching victory from the jaws of defeat. The sword techniques Ittōsai employed in that incident were taught to his most senior disciple, Mikogami Tenzen, as Ittō-ryū's secret *Hosshatō* techniques, and they have been passed on to successive generations ever since.

Ittōsai met with calamity that night, deeply reflected on this, and was ashamed of his blunder, and aside from being fooled from the start by those who became his students and benefitted from his lessons, he was troubled that he wasn't able to gain their respect while teaching them face-to-face, and that his inability to inspire them is what led to this act of mutiny. Determined more than ever to improve his own character, he decided to escape from the world of pleasure that permeated the capital and, with the firm resolve to devote himself entirely to the perfection of Ittō-ryū, left Kyoto that night, heading east before the break of dawn. Those of later generations who learned Hosshatō not only acquired the superb martial techniques to cut through enemies surrounding them from all sides, but through it also inevitably comprehended his significant contribution of opening a path to a new mental state of being prepared to lay everything on the line[58] by sweeping away delusions caused by the impetuousness and distractions that come from the pursuit of hedonistic pleasure.

Ittōsai deeply reflected on how he let down his guard that evening and this event constituted a major turning point in his life. Even though he had an innate genius [with the sword], if he couldn't control his hot-blooded impulses or transcend them, there was no way he would ever be able to make his way in the world as a master swordsman. Ittōsai experienced a time of youthful exuberance that all young people go through, but once he put his finger on the problem, he took the view that he would only be able to live an extraordinary life by practicing self-discipline. He pondered this even more and continued his efforts to foster the supernatural ability to sense impending danger anywhere and anytime.

He refined an acute ability to predict the weather and natural disasters as well as an intuitive insight into the fundamental nature of people. As a consequence, he had nerves of steel, and in the end, whether asleep or awake, he never lost his head, whether in a crisis or the times he was focused on only one task, never failed to defend to the rear when he was attacking to his front, and

47

was completely prepared for anything, anywhere, at any time. It was from this that Ittō-ryū's esoteric lessons of *Scratching an Itch, Dealing with Whatever Comes,*[59] *Tetsujō-tekka* (徹上徹下), *Making an Ally of All Things,*[60] the *Grass Pillow, One Sword is Many Swords,*[61] and the lesson that we must not forget war in times of peace are derived.

Taking on Ono Zenki as an Attendant

One evening, as he was approaching Kuwama in Ise after setting out alone on a journey without any particular purpose, Ittōsai availed himself of a ferry that happened to be leaving that night to take him across the sea.[§] The sky illuminated the water, the reflection of the full moon bobbed among the waves, and the cool of the night gave a crisp chill all around. There were many other passengers boarding the boat besides Ittōsai. Ittōsai filed onto the ferry with them, selected a seat in a corner, and sat upright in a meditative posture. Before long, the boat slipped away from the bank and into the sea bathed in the pale moonlight. The sound of the ferryman's oar passing through the water broke the night silence and marked time while a cool breeze blew. The passengers on the boat breathed in the refreshing night air. Ittōsai, enthralled by the water and sky around him, experienced the sculling with clarity of mind and became one with the mystic atmosphere of the seas, mountains, and stars. As the boat slipped further out to sea it crested higher and higher waves, but none of the passengers uttered a sound. Ittōsai soon calmed his mind, got in tune with the rhythm of the oar in the water, and was in a state of mental detachment[62] when he suddenly felt a disturbance in the rhythm

---

[§] There is an alternate theory that this incident took place on the calm part of a river.

48

of the ferryman's sculling. When he happened to glance over at him, his eyes met the ferryman's across the boat. The oarsman was powerfully built, standing over six feet tall, with arms like a gorilla's. His face was gnarled in a churlish expression. When their eyes met, the ferryman suddenly stopped rowing and turned toward him, saying, "By all appearances, honorable customer, you carry yourself with great dignity and are holding a wooden sword. You must be a distinguished warrior. I, on the other hand, am but a lowly ferryman, but ever since I was a kid I have dabbled in the martial arts. I have always looked forward to meeting a warrior who knows something about them and requesting a 'lesson.'[63] I would like to ask for one now."

With just a glance, Ittōsai could see in the ferryman a vicious streak, his solid frame, and his crude skills, but feigned ignorance and tried to ignore him. The ferryman pressed his point home by grabbing a nearby bundle of three-inch-thick "iron-hollow" Chinese bamboo in one hand and crushing the stalks together with a crunch. His fearlessness and pride in his Herculean strength showed on his face when he said, "So far, of those I faced who called themselves samurai, not one could stand up to my powerful techniques. Is that silly wooden sword meant to be intimidating? That kind of thing is no match for me. If you are up to it, face me in a square fight and let's see."

He raised his voice as he drew nearer. Ittōsai didn't let this insolence bother him, for if he had allowed himself to get indignant the oarsman would have just imposed one unreasonable demand after another on the other passengers around him and caused them no end of trouble. To teach the ferryman a lesson, to spare inconveniencing the other passengers, and also thinking he would enjoy the evening, he replied, "Well then, I will grant your request to have a match. But let's go to the shore so we don't trouble the other passengers."

The ferryman jumped at the idea and excitedly steered to the nearest beach with violent splashes of his oar. He was the first on land. While keeping his eye on the ferryman, Ittōsai followed suit and alighted. The passengers in the boat all clambered out and watched with breathless anticipation.

The ferryman took hold of a large oar about twelve feet long, faced Ittōsai, and raised it high overhead. Ittōsai matched this with his own sword held in a high posture. The ferryman inched toward Ittōsai, eager to strike, but Ittōsai's posture, using the principle of *Action in Waiting*, [64] allowed not the slightest of openings, while his dignified demeanor and presence pierced straight through the ferryman, rattling him to the core. While the boatman held the oar high overhead, he was unable to do anything at all. After one breath, two breaths, there was absolutely no opportunity to cut, no matter what. He started gasping for breath, his head started to swim, and when he finally couldn't take it anymore, he brought the oar down with a roar toward the top of Ittōsai's head to crush it, relying on his superhuman strength. From Ittōsai's perspective, the ferryman's strike, like his stance, was riddled with weak points and went far off the mark, striking thin air. While watching all this, Ittōsai moved toward the ferryman and brought his sword down hard on his right forearm. The ferryman let out a scream as his oar went flying and landed on the island where it stuck in the ground. The ferryman fell to the ground on the spot and prostrated himself in front of Ittōsai.

"For many years I have earned a living as a lowly ferryman so I could seek out a worthy teacher among the passengers I carried. Now, my wish has finally been fulfilled. How about it? Can you take me on as a student and teach me?" he implored.

When he heard this, Ittōsai's first order of business was to admonish the boatman for his insolence and the second was to accept his request and permit him to accompany him on his travels as his personal attendant. [65]

The ferryman's name at the time was Chōshichi,[66] but after the duel he changed it to Ono Zenki. And because he accompanied Ittōsai on his travels around Japan, he built upon his natural talent and developed even greater skill, becoming the best of all of Ittōsai's students. Thenceforth, whenever Ittōsai received a challenge from someone, he normally had Zenki meet them first to see how good they were, but there were none who ever bested him.

Zenki trained under Ittōsai for many years, but in the end his innate vile and greedy temperament was irredeemable. He conceived of the treasonously sinister idea that if he could just get rid of Ittōsai he himself would be celebrated as the best swordsman in the land, so he came up with a scheme to murder his teacher in the middle of the night while he was asleep. But Ittōsai had such a high level of supernatural ability to sense danger that he figured this out, and the years passed without him ever giving Zenki the opportunity to act. While seeing through Zenki's depravity and knowing about the danger to himself, Ittōsai also recognized Zenki's superior talent and hoped that, in due course, he would mend his ways. With this magnanimous attitude, as well as with the sober understanding of what he was getting into, he allowed Zenki to remain under his tutelage.

Stopping the Jizuri-no-Seigan Technique

In the eastern provinces there was a man who excelled with the sword. He used his own specially developed sword technique he had perfected over many years called the *Jizuri-no-Seigan* when he engaged in duels, and no one ever defeated it. He heard of Ittōsai's reputation and, wanting to request a match to see if Ittōsai could stop his special technique, happily went to meet him when he heard he was travelling east from Kyoto. Ittōsai first had

51

Zenki accept the challenge, but the match was a draw. Afraid he might miss his chance with Ittōsai, he invited him to stay in the room next to his and rolled out the red carpet.

After staying at the inn for a few days, Ittōsai observed the fellow and determined he wasn't up to the task of receiving a "lesson," so he decided to head off to another province. On his way out, he stopped by the Tsurugaoka Hachiman Shrine to pray and was taking a break in the main hall of worship. That's when the man showed up, saw that Ittōsai was about to leave for another domain, and boasted that Ittōsai was surely trying to slip away because he knew deep down that he couldn't defend against his unique sword tactic. Raising his voice, the man shouted, "Ignoring my challenge to you to stop my *Jizuri-no-Seigan* technique that I've been requesting day after day and accepting an invitation to go to another province is unconscionable. If you don't grant my request at this time, I'll never get another chance. I ask that you provide this lesson here and now!" With that, he whipped out his sword and shot in with his special tactic to cut down Ittōsai.

Ittōsai was sitting on a stone tying the laces of his sandals, and no sooner did he see the sword slashing toward him that he cleaved the man in two where he stood as quick as a flash. Ittōsai didn't think twice, calmly got up, and left as if nothing had happened. How to stop the *Jizuri-no-Seigan* was a lesson the man learned with his life. There are those who regret that none of his successors were ever taught how he stopped this technique, but what Ittōsai was considering at the time wasn't such things as how his opponent was poised to execute his special technique, he was thinking of nothing more than sweeping away a wicked sword of pride that barred his progress along the Way with a single, decisive cut.[67] With that in mind, he just moved forward and let his sword do the rest. Whenever Ittōsai engaged in major life or death duels, once he won, he never looked back. There was not one iota of desire within him to cling to the past. Once he took that first step there was no going back, and he never stopped in his quest to seek boundless improvement.

Ittōsai's Duels with Other Famous Swordsmen

There were many famous warriors Ittōsai defeated in combat. When he visited the province of Shinshū, he challenged Tsukuhara Bokuden, the founder of Tenshin Shoden Shinto-ryū and considered the best swordsman of his day. Bokuden was famous at the time of the duel, and no matter how Ittōsai tried to attack or find weaknesses in his guard, Bokuden left no openings. Suddenly, Ittōsai struck toward Bokuden and knelt down on one knee. Then, just when Bokuden started to cut toward him, Ittōsai stood up while thrusting his own sword over Bokuden's hands, stopping his cut and stabbing him in the process, beating him. This is a move in the Orimi technique of the Odachi kata that has been taught to students ever since.

When Ittōsai arrived in the domain of Jōshū, he fought a duel against Morooka Ippa of the Mijin-ryū[68] and beat him on the spot. He also traveled to the province of Kishū and defeated the distinguished warrior Arima Yamato-no-Kami Kiminobu of the Kashima Shin-ryū.[69] After that, Ittōsai appeared in the province of Kōshū and won another duel against the famous Kamiizumi Ise-no-Kami Nobutsuna of the Shinkage-ryū,[70] and then went to the province of Jōshū, where he fought and defeated the renowned Okano Hyuga of the Toda-ryū.[71] Whenever Ittōsai faced an opponent, he beat him with only a single cut and never crossed swords a second time. This is because when he faced them, he first attacked them with his mind and ki, and right after he defeated them with these, he struck them down with a single stroke of his sword.

The five people above who were defeated by Ittōsai were famous sword masters in their own right, but even though they were beaten by him they didn't become his students because they were the heads of their own schools. It was the custom of the day, however, for those who had been defeated to hand over to Ittōsai all of the secrets of their schools they had hidden away. Of course, once they lost to Ittōsai, the secret techniques of their schools had to be revealed. Ittōsai exploited his victories over these masters by compiling the techniques he used to defeat them within Ittō-ryū's kumitachi as the Taryūkachi-no-kata, which has been passed down generation after generation.

Aside from the five famous sword masters above, there were many others whom Ittōsai defeated and who later became students: Itō Magobe,[72] Ogura Ichigaku,[73] Mamiya Shinzaemon,[74] Takatsu Ichizaemon,[75] Kotoda Kageyuzaemon Toshinao,[76] Ono Zenki,[77] and Mikogami Tenzen Yoshiaki.[78] Among these, the one who rose above the rest to become Ittōsai's personal attendant, trained the hardest, received the highest-level secrets, and succeeded him as the next headmaster of Ittō-ryū, was Mikogami Tenzen. He would later change his name to Ono Jirōemon Tadaaki.

Another of those who tested their skills against Ittōsai was a man who hailed from China named Jukkan.[79] Starting in the Hojo period (1199-1333), ships from China received approval to trade with Japan. A master of Chinese martial arts named Jukkan set sail on one of these boats, landed at the port city of Miura-Misaki on July 2, 1578, and challenged the samurai warriors of Japan to a test of skills, but not one responded.

Jukkan unsheathed the gleaming blade of his halberd to display his martial prowess. He stood over six feet tall, with a powerful build and a piercing gaze. He cut an imposing figure, with the bristles of his beard standing straight out like a tiger's whiskers. He slipped his arms out of the long, flowing sleeves of his shirt and made a dramatic entrance into a large garden wearing a hakama bloused around his ankles. The power he displayed when he readied his halberd was awe-inspiring. He did a solo performance of his martial art for about an hour, acting as if he was defeating his enemies in mortal combat. He twirled his weapon, glared with wild eyes, clenched his teeth, shouted, and kicked up clouds of dust as he moved this way and that, slashing in all directions, chasing imaginary enemies around and vigorously cutting them all down. People were fixated by this display and marveled at his skill. By chance, Ittōsai happened upon this spectacle when he overheard everyone talking up Jukkan, saying things like, "Even someone like Ittōsai, who calls himself the greatest in Japan, would not dare show his face here." Thinking that letting this challenge go unanswered would bring dishonor to the Japanese martial arts, he rose to the occasion and accepted a match against Jukkan. The crowd of onlookers was delighted.**

After both finished preparing, they strode into the wide garden where the match would take place. They faced each other, with Jukkan brandishing a wooden halberd, while Ittōsai held only a single folding fan. Jukkan was fully on guard and faced Ittōsai with a menacing posture, poised to employ his most secret techniques while carefully looking for the right time to strike. Watching this, Ittōsai waited for the optimal moment, tossed away his fan, and faced Jukkan with his arms spread wide open. Seeing this strange display, Jukkan reacted very cautiously, firmly pointing the sharp tip of his blade at Ittōsai and inching forward in the attack. When Jukkan suddenly took a step forward, Ittōsai took one step back. When Ittōsai spread his hands and shuffled forward, Jukkan shuffled back.

** There is an alternate theory that the person in this story facing Jukkan was someone other than Ittōsai.

When one side closed in to the right, the other shifted to the left. When one attacked from the left, the other evaded to the right. When one drove the other across the garden, the other reversed the situation, circling around in the attack. It was impossible to tell who was winning and who was losing. The fight went on this way for a long time until Ittōsai, spotting a golden opportunity, jumped forward in a flash and kicked down the handle of Jukkan's halberd. Not just Jukkan, but the on-lookers as well, were astonished and struck dumb by such a nimble and quick feat of agility. Ittōsai remained completely unruffled as he spread both hands over the prostrated Jukkan and brought the contest to a close.

The Miracle of Musōken

Having been blessed as a warrior with unparalleled natural ability, over the span of many years, Ittōsai mustered up his courage, risked death, devoted himself to developing sword techniques used in duels, went through trials and tribulations, and taxed his ingenuity in training. Ultimately, he lived up to the reputation he earned as the best swordsman in Japan, but he went even further, wracking his brains in the endless pursuit of the inner secrets of swordsmanship without an ounce of conceit.

However, after exhausting all other avenues and not being able to grasp the divine truth [80] that got to the heart of the profundity of swordsmanship, he shut himself up in the Tsurugaoka Hachimangu Shrine in the Sagami Domain for seven days, seeking divine guidance. Day and night he fervently prayed, but by the dawning of the last day his efforts had come to naught. The divine revelation still eluded him. Just as he started to leave the prayer area, he sensed the approach of an evil spirit creeping up from behind to attack, and without conscious thought and without saying a word, drew his sword and cut toward it, cleaving the apparition completely in two. Years of delusional thoughts he had clung to immediately vanished into thin air, and he recalled achieving a state of mind that was free, bright, and clear. Ittōsai related this incident to his students the next day, saying he was able to easily achieve victory by reacting without conscious effort using No-Mind[81] and moving without effort like mist effortlessly flowing around obstacles,[82] and that he was able to achieve a state of eternal peace and tranquility after sweeping it away. This was when he was able to get his first great insight into the highest-level secret of Musōken.[83]

Enlightenment in Ittōsai's Twilight Years

While Itō Ittōsai traversed the various domains of Japan, his fights with the steel sword numbered thirty-three, the powerful opponents he killed numbered fifty-seven, the number he struck down with a wooden sword was sixty-two, and the various acts of goodwill he performed were incalculable. As a warrior, Ittōsai was unrivaled in all of Japan but he never put down roots. He traveled all over the land with the mind of a great warrior looking for other worthy opponents against whom to test his skills, and whenever someone challenged him – requesting a "lesson" – he unflinchingly accepted.

Once when Ittōsai was staying in Bishū, Oda Nobunaga heard of his reputation and approached him with a generous proposal, but Ittōsai, having no interest in receiving a stipend or serving a daimyo, did not respond to this overture. So, Nobunaga sent another envoy who implored:

"We are at a critical juncture in these turbulent times, so we definitely want you to come. If there is a worthy man among your disciples who has a mind to serve as your representative, we would like you to bestow upon him the superb techniques of your school and have him enter into the service of our lord."

After listening to Nobunaga's entreaty, Ittōsai agreed. He assigned one of his most able students the surname of Itō, bestowed upon him the highest-level secrets of the school, and let him serve Nobunaga as Itō Tenzen.

There were times when Ittōsai struck out on solitary journeys, leaving his students behind, avoiding others, and looking forward to communing with nature. He spent many a night in the rooms of broken-down country hovels. Once, when he opened his eyes in the middle of the night in one of these huts, his eye met a shaft of moonlight. Gazing serenely at the beam of light streaming in, he felt he could read the intention of the moon. Though the moon shone down upon the entire roof, if there were even the tiniest of holes in it, a shaft of moonlight would shoot through it directly into his room. This became the basis for the idea that, while observing all parts of your opponent, if there is even the tiniest of openings, that is the spot where you shoot in just like a shaft of moonlight. This is how Ittōsai came to understand the tactic of *Kurai of Moonlight*, in which one sharpens his own mind, calms it, and then uses it to illuminate his opponent's action.

He journeyed to Suntō and faced Mt. Fugaku[84] many times. He traveled around to the eight sacred peaks that stood majestic against the azure sky and established the lesson of *Looking at the Mountain*[85] after observing the clouds circulating around them, never stopping day or night. He also expounded upon the principle of the *Deer*[86] after watching the actions of a hunter as he stalked a deer in a plain below. When he observed a fox being chased by a dog, he developed the lesson of the *Doubting Mind of a Fox*.[87] While taking shelter on the leeward side of an old pine tree after encountering a raging storm on the road to Hakone, he developed the principle of *Wind Through the Pine Trees*[88] based on the sound of the wind blowing through its branches. And while passing through Musashino, he saw how reeds and branches of willow trees gently swayed in the breeze and took their undulations away as a deep secret.

Even though he was soon without a rival who could have challenged him, he continued to devote himself to the study of the sword, made Mother Nature his teacher throughout the rest of his life, communed with the sun, moon, and stars that make up the heavenly bodies rotating in the sky,[89] studied Heaven-Earth-Yin-Yang theory, put his heart and soul into the philosophical principle of *All Things in the Universe are as One,* and imbued all of these lessons into the One Sword where they became ordering principles when he created and formalized Ittō-ryū. As he entered his twilight years, he eschewed his hard-earned reputation, passed on all of the inner secrets of his school to Mikogami Tenzen Yoshiaki, and by so doing, laid the groundwork for his art to be passed on to future generations. This was around the time Toyotomi Hideyoshi unified the land and returned the country to an era of peace, but Ittōsai parted ways with Yoshiaki in Shimōsa and simply disappeared. The date was August 7, 1591. After that, Ittōsai left worldly affairs behind and took the tonsure, kept his new name a secret, silently meditated while praying for the eternal peace of the dead, and lived out the rest of his life in tranquility as he pursued spiritual salvation.

Itō Ittōsai Kagehisa, the model samurai, civic-minded hero, sage who rejected worldly desires, and sword-saint incarnate, went into seclusion in his later years and left no reliable record of where he died. Mikogami Tenzen Yoshiaki, later called Ono Jirōemon Tadaaki, who received the entire lineage of Ittō-ryū from Ittōsai, decided that August 7th, the day he parted with his beloved teacher forever,[††] would be the day he would honor the memory of Itō Ittōsai and perform memorial rights for him.

[††] There is an alternate theory that he passed away on June 20, 1654.

(Note): Ittōsai's surname has been written in various ways throughout history, such as: 伊藤, 井藤, 伊東, and 井東. This is because people in the past who recorded his name were careless about which Chinese characters they used and passed them on incorrectly. The spelling of Itō Ittōsai Kagehisa (伊藤一刀齋景久) presented herein has been confirmed in the catalogues of the highest-level secrets [90] passed down from the founder and maintained within the House of Tsugaru.

Endnotes to Chapter Two

[39] *Sandan no kurai* (三段の位)

[40] *Butokuden* (武徳殿)

[41] Also known as Mutsu-no-Kami Minamoto Yoshiie.

[42] *Godan no kurai* (五段の位)

[43] *Kongō* (金剛)

[44] *Shukyō sanmai* (宗教三昧)

[45] *Kongotō* (金剛刀)

[46] *Chūdachi* (中太刀)

[47] *Bokutō* (木刀).

[48] *Hankan-ryū* (判官流). This school was also known as Hangan-ryū and Okuyama Nen-ryū.

[49] *Shinken* (真剣)

[50] *Nyoi* (鉄如意). Nyoi, which were originally used as back-scratchers, were later used as crosiers of priests in Buddhism.

[51] *Kiketsu* (気血)

[52] *Kenshin ichinyo* (剣心一如の妙理)

[53] *Isshintō* (一心刀)

[54] *Hisei ittai banbutsu no ichinyo* (彼成一体万物一如)

[55] Transliterated as the *One Sword School*.

[56] *Iyoku tantan toshite mizu no gotoku* (意欲淡々として水の如く)

[57] *Hosshatō* (払捨刀)

[58] *Daishi ichiban* (大死一番)

[59] *Happō bunshin* (八方分身)

[60] *Banbutsu mikata kokore* (万物味方心得)

[61] *Ittō-sunawachi-bantō* (一刀即万刀)

[62] *Mugamushin no sakai* (無我無心の境)

[63] Asking for a "lesson" was a euphemistic way of challenging someone to a duel in this period of Japan.

[64] *Action in Waiting* is a set of skills explained in more detail in later volumes of this book series.

[65] *Zuishin* (髄身)

[66] *Chōshichi* (長七)

[67] *Ittō no Ichimonji* (一刀の一文字)

[68] Mijin-ryū (微塵流)

⁶⁹ Kashima Shin-ryū (鹿島神流)

⁷⁰ Shinkage-ryū (新陰流)

⁷¹ Toda-ryū (富田流)

⁷² Itō Magobe (伊藤弥兵衛)

⁷³ Ogura Ichigaku (小倉一学)

⁷⁴ Mamiya Shinzaemon (間宮新左衛門)

⁷⁵ Takatsu Ichizaemon (高津市左衛門)

⁷⁶ Kotoda Kageyuzaemon Toshinao (古藤田勘解由衛門俊直)

⁷⁷ Ono Zenki (小野善鬼)

⁷⁸ Mikogami Tenzen Yoshiaki (神子上典膳吉明)

⁷⁹ *Jukkan* (十官)

⁸⁰ *Shintei* (神諦)

⁸¹ *Mushin* (無心)

⁸² *Rurō jizai* (流霞自在)

⁸³ *Musōken* (夢想剣)

⁸⁴ Another name for Mt. Fuji.

⁸⁵ *Miyama/Kenzan* (見山)

⁸⁶ *Shika no koto* (鹿の事)

⁸⁷ *Kōgishin* (狐疑心)

⁸⁸ *Matsukaze* (松風)

⁸⁹ *Tenkōken* (天行建)

⁹⁰ *Gokui mokuroku* (極意目録)

CHAPTER THREE

Life of Ono Jirōemon Tadaaki

Ittōsai Takes on Tenzen as a Student

Mikogami Tenzen Yoshiaki, who later changed his name to Ono Jirōemon Tadaaki, hailed from Ise and can trace his lineage through his ancestors to Toichi Hyobu-no-kami, a castellan in the Yamato Domain. Tenzen was born in 1565 as the third son of Mikogami Tosa-no-kami. He later moved to Kazusa Province and served the House of Mangi no Shōhitsu. Tenzen was a man of moral courage and showed a talent for the martial arts from when he was a child. By the time he was a young man, he stood head and shoulders above his peers and had occasion to rely on the fencing skills of the Mikami-ryu, which he had studied for many years. One day, Itō Ittōsai Kagehisa, whose martial exploits were known far and wide, happened to go to Kazusa and put up a large sign-board in front of his inn that said: *If there is anyone in this domain who wants a lesson in fencing, come and challenge me.* Tenzen, thinking he had a golden opportunity to test the skills that he had been developing day-by-day, went to meet Ittōsai at his inn and requested a match. Ittōsai accepted on the spot.

When the time came for the duel, Tenzen pulled out his sword and faced Ittōsai, ready for action, while Ittōsai nonchalantly pulled an eighteen-inch piece of charred firewood out of a fire pit and faced him. Tenzen took up a wakigamae stance with his thirty-three-and-a-half-inch blade[91] signed by Namihira Yukiyasu and closed in for the kill, but Ittōsai effortlessly disarmed him, set his sword on a stack of firewood nearby, and went back inside the inn. Tenzen just stood there, stupefied, but after coming to his senses, asked for one more try.

Ittōsai emerged from the inn, saying: "Practice is important for those who are young, so I will be your training partner as many times as you want. I won't try to hurt you so just come at me."

With that, Ittōsai picked up the same piece of firewood he used before, but this time Tenzen picked up a wooden training sword about three feet long. Tenzen cut in with all his might, but no matter where he cut, his sword was knocked down every time. He couldn't even touch Ittōsai's clothes.

At a complete loss, he went home. Reflecting all night long on what happened, he was struck with awe, marveling at how Ittōsai was like water, moving like a divine being. Could he have been some kind of guardian spirit?

He made up his mind to learn from Ittōsai and returned to the inn the next day, prostrated himself, and begged to become his student. Ittōsai saw the desire within this young warrior, recognized his sincerity and innate genius, and saw that he had a bright future, so he accepted his request. Tenzen was ecstatic and started to study under Ittōsai. The eighteen-and-a-half-inch[92] short sword used in Ittō-ryū today is based on the length of the piece of firewood Ittōsai used that day.

Shortly thereafter, Ittōsai departed Kazusa for other provinces but returned the next year to visit Tenzen. Tenzen happily welcomed him and enthusiastically trained at his feet. Ittōsai cherished the rare talent of Tenzen. Moreover, after seeing how hard he worked and realizing that he was certain to achieve great things in the future, he approached him, saying:

"From today onward, if you want to get ahead in life and make a name for yourself through mastering the highest secrets of this school, you should come along with me as I visit the various provinces on a warrior pilgrimage.[93] It would be a good way to test yourself, build your character, and polish your techniques."

Tenzen was inspired by Ittōsai's encouragement and decided deep in his heart to go. He soon accompanied Ittōsai as his attendant[94] as he toured Japan's many domains, built up his skills, and when they met any famous sword masters, Tenzen would face them first or would watch as Ittōsai faced them in duels and learn from him. He gradually mastered both the physical and mental aspects of the art.

Fight to the Death Between Tenzen and Zenki

For quite some time before, Ittōsai already had a personal attendant, Ono Zenki, who stood out for his herculean strength and tremendous technical skill, but due to his brutish and arrogant nature he didn't live up to Ittōsai's expectations. Instead, Ittōsai placed his confidence in Mikogami Tenzen and held a secret desire to pass on the school of Ittō-ryū to him. One day Ittōsai called Tenzen close to his side.

"Today I have decided to pass on to you the documents containing the deepest secrets of our discipline so you can inherit the school of Ittō-ryū and pass it on to future generations. However, there is the issue of Zenki, who has been my attendant before you. Because your skills aren't up to his, I will pass on to you a tactic that will ensure your victory. Use it in your fight, if you wish" he confided. With that, Ittōsai bestowed upon Tenzen the Kamewari sword that had never left his side along with the secret tactic of Musōken.

On the appointed day, Ittōsai, who was pushing old age, went with both Zenki and Tenzen to the Somagahara Plain* in the Shimōsa Domain and announced to both:

> From when I was young, I practiced the military arts, roamed all over this land, visited all of those in my day who had made a name for themselves in the martial arts, and none of those I challenged could ever beat me. After that, I honored the gods in heaven, kept company with the stars in the sky, imbued the Way of Yin-Yang of the Great Ultimate into the sword, and compiled the curriculum of Ittō-ryū, and by doing so, laid the groundwork to pass it on in perpetuity. At long last, I have completed what I set out to do and have no other aspirations. Besides, I feel old age has already crept up on me. So, here and now I have decided to pass on all of the secrets of Ittō-ryū to one of you and have you take over the school. But, due to the code that says only one person can be the successor,[95] I am not able to bestow this school upon two people. Since I am only going to pass it on to the one who is the better fighter, you two will decide through honorable combat here, on this wide open plain, who it will be.

Zenki implored that since he was the most senior student the honor should fall to him, but Ittōsai would hear none of it. At that, Zenki suddenly snatched away the documents containing the secrets of Ittō-ryū sitting next to Ittōsai and took off running at full speed. Ittōsai and Tenzen chased after him. Zenki, not able to get

---

* There is an alternate explanation that this occurred on the Kuritsuwara Plain (栗津原).

away, spotted a large earthenware urn under the boughs of a pine tree and crawled under it to hide. Tenzen ran up to it and started pushing it away. Ittōsai, running a bit slower due to his age, saw what Tenzen was doing from a distance and shouted:

"If you move the urn out of the way, your legs will be slashed. Cut through both!"

As soon as Tenzen heard this, he sliced through the urn in one powerful cut, lopping Zenki's head clean off. This was where Tenzen first comprehended the mysteries of *kiai*.[96] Though Zenki's head was severed from his body, his eyes were wide open and he held the secret documents firmly clenched in his teeth, not letting go. Ittōsai witnessed this, and though Zenki was a despicable character, he sympathized with his passion for pursuing the Way. He tried to console him, saying:

"I chose you first to receive Ittō-ryū's secrets, but later decided to bestow them upon Tenzen."

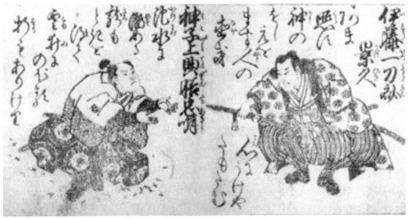

Ittōsai bestows the Kamewaritō sword and secret documents of Ittō-ryū to Tadaaki.

When Zenki heard this, a smile went across his face, he released the secret documents from his teeth, and he died contented. Even today there is a burial mound for Zenki in

67

Koganehara, Soma District, Shimōsa Province, and people from all over call the pine tree that's next to it the *Zenki Pine*.[97]

Tenzen had been by Ittōsai's side and diligently applied himself to the mastery of Ittō-ryū for many years, but up to that point he had always been one notch below his senior, Zenki. But this time around he was handed the way to Certain Victory from his teacher, and due to this gracious act, defeated Zenki, whereupon he was awarded the treasured Kamewari Ichimonji sword, along with the highest-level secrets of Ittō-ryū that could only be passed on to one person. Though he was appointed the inheritor of Ittō-ryū, he fell to his knees overcome by sadness and prayed while choked up with tears of gratitude as he watched his aged and revered teacher fade away in the distance after announcing he was leaving forever.

Tenzen Goes to Edo

Mikogami Tenzen Yoshiaki parted ways with his beloved teacher, from whom he spent many years learning. Ittōsai's lessons were deeply ingrained in his mind when he returned to his native land of Kazusa. The youngsters of his hometown heard of his return, and many gathered to welcome him home, became his students, and received splendid lessons from him. But true genius won't be hidden for long, and not wanting to while away his time hanging around a humble backwater, he took every word and phrase of his esteemed teacher to heart and eventually set out on his own like his master to introduce to the world the school of Ittō-ryū he had learned. The burning ambition to make it a priceless treasure for all generations of warriors[98] welled up from deep within his heart, and he made up his mind to leave his ancestral home and travel alone to Edo in the Musashi Domain.

The Edo of that time was the new location of the capital that Tokugawa Ieyasu had just relocated from Sunpu, and while it was called a "castle town," the bleak remains of the downfall of the Hojo and the post-conflict desolation that remained permeated the place, which was just a minor outpost in a desolate spot sandwiched between water and land and dotted here and there with a few farm huts and fisherman's hovels. Ieyasu formed his government and wasted no time rebuilding what was destroyed during the hostilities. It was a time when he mustered troops, gradually restored law and order, dispatched officials to re-establish a bureaucracy, determined the layout of the city, and worked hard to entice merchants and artisans, all the while striving to create the foundation of a capital of the Eastern provinces.

Tenzen traveled to Edo, visited the districts that were thriving, and made his way to the Kanda district. When he climbed the heights of Surugadai and took in the view, there were only a few merchant houses interspersed within shouting distance of each other facing the reeds swaying in the wind in the salty marshes. The lushness of the Musashino Plateau spread out before him, and he could barely recognize the hills that undulated far off in the distance. Tenzen surveyed this scene, formed a picture in his mind of how the capital city would develop, and became excited about how he might capitalize on these expansions. He climbed down from the high ground, searched for lodging when he reached the Hatago Machi,[99] and found a small place where he took up temporary residence.

The Scion of the One Sword – Top School in the Land

Tenzen hung an audacious sign in front of his place that read: *Mikogami Tenzen, the Scion of the One Sword – the Best School in the Land. Those who wish to test their skills, inquire within.* Around the time Tenzen arrived in Edo, sentiment for Toyotomi Hideyoshi was still strong. His son Hideyori was still a boy in Osaka, and rival warlords, who were eyeing the situation, were still firmly entrenched in every part of Japan while the tide of public sentiment had yet to turn in favor of the Tokugawa, who were holed up in Edo. This was around the time that Tokugawa Ieyasu squared off against Maeda Toshiie, and while eagerly awaiting the right time to pounce, began assembling under his command an impressive constellation of distinguished and formidable warriors. Among them, Okubo Hikozaemon, Yokota Jirobei, Nagasaka Nobumasa,[100] and Obata Kanbei Kagenori stood out for their battlefield exploits. Because Mikogami Tenzen, a no-name country rōnin, hung such an outrageously insolent signboard in the middle of the Tokugawa army's main stronghold, it soon created a wide stir and reached the ears of Tokugawa's *hatamotos*,[101] who couldn't stomach such arrogance. They started to talk about a test of skills when they had a chance.

At that juncture a number of hatamotos gathered in Obata Kanbei's residence in Kanda Surugadai and talked about martial arts. Kanbei spoke up: "I've been informed that a cocky fellow in Hatago Machi named Mikogami Tenzen put out a signboard that said he was the best swordsman in the land. We shouldn't just ignore this. Fortunately, he is not far from my home, so I think I will pay him a visit tomorrow morning to test him and see what happens." Everyone agreed it was a good idea.

The next day, Kanbei finished his breakfast before dawn, walked to the inn district where Tenzen was staying, and called out his name. Tenzen, looking as if he had just woken up, met him wrapped in a flimsy robe. Kanbei challenged him, saying, "I have come to answer your request for a match as per the signboard hanging in front of your quarters."

"I am quite happy to accept. But since I haven't had my morning meal yet, I ask that you wait a little while," Tenzen replied.

He made Kanbei wait while he put rice in a copper kettle and boiled it into gruel. After he quietly ate it all, he turned to Kanbei.

"Since you are the renowned Lord Obata Kanbei Kagenori, I will leave it up to you to decide what we should use: sharpened steel, blunted swords, wooden practice swords, or something else," he said.

"Let's use wooden swords," Kanbei replied, grabbing a mid-length sword[102] while standing up. Tenzen secured an eighteen-inch piece of firewood from a fire pit, stood up, and they both squared off.

From his very first strike, Kanbei hit with all his might, trying to land a blow, but never managed to touch him, and no matter how he attacked, wasn't able to beat him. Tenzen, not fazed in the least, knew how to handle all of Kanbei's moves. Seeing this, Kanbei realized that he was no match for Tenzen, put away his weapon, and bowed deeply, saying: "Lord Tenzen's miraculous techniques truly defy description. I beseech you to allow me to become your student and learn this skill."

He pledged his loyalty to Tenzen and left. At a meeting with his fellow hatamoto afterwards, Kanbei described in detail Tenzen's tremendous skill, publicly proclaimed how he was truly a top-notch swordsman, and said that everyone should seek him out as their teacher.

Tenzen's Showdown with Munenori

At this time in Edo, the one who enjoyed the reputation as the greatest of all swordsmen was Yagyu Tajima-no-Kami Munenori.[103] It was only natural that Tenzen would want to meet him once for a showdown. One day Tenzen searched for Munenori's estate and asked a local inn keeper where his residence might be. The inn keeper was suspicious and asked what business he had with Munenori. When Tenzen replied that he wanted to request a match, the inn keeper held back his surprise.

"There are those who go to the Yagyu mansion and request duels every now and then, but so far no one has ever lived to return home. It would be best if you gave up and spared yourself," he warned.

Hearing this, Tenzen said, "I hear that Lord Yagyu isn't just a superior martial artist but a benevolent and gracious man as well. I dare say he wouldn't kill someone for no reason. Surely he'd have a good justification for doing that." Unable to convince the inn keeper to help, he searched around and eventually found the Yagyu mansion and requested a duel with Munenori through an intermediary.

Tenzen's challenge was accepted and he was granted permission to enter the mansion but had to surrender his two swords[104] at the entrance. He was ushered into the dojo where he was made to wait. After an eternity, Munenori finally showed up, removed his *kataginu*,[105] pulled out a sword and approached him saying, "According to the code of our school, those who request a match with Munenori agree to fight to the death. If you have anything to say, you can say it now."

While Tenzen had been waiting in the dojo he had investigated his environs inside and out and happened to spot a handy eighteen-inch piece of firewood in a fire pit outside. He darted out an open door, grabbed it, and returned to the dojo.

"I think I'll let this do my talking," he said while squaring off with Munenori.

Munenori at first brushed off this remark with a contemptuous look, but after realizing how surprisingly tough his opponent would be, he pulled himself together and started cutting with all of his might, but Tenzen didn't go down as expected. Munenori, red in the face, fought furiously, unleashing all of the secret techniques of Shinkage-ryū in a desperate attempt to cut him, but couldn't land a single blow. All the while, Tenzen's strikes rained down all over his head and shoulders – he was pounded everywhere until his clothing became stained black from the charcoal on the piece of firewood Tenzen was holding. Munenori's heart started pounding as if he had his back against the wall. He was so out of breath he could barely speak, and he was sopping in sweat while Tenzen was calm and collected and quiet as a deep abyss. Seeing this, Munenori was deeply impressed. He sheathed his sword and called over his shoulder for Tenzen to wait for a while as he left.

Still wearing his charcoal-stained clothes, he went to the castle where he met with Okubo Hikozaemon, gave him a detailed account, and recommended that if he were to hire Tenzen he would make a good palanquin guard [106] for the House of Tokugawa. Hikozaemon had only recently started hearing about the superior sword skills of this guy Tenzen, whom Obata Kagenori had been talking up, and reported this to Tokugawa Ieyasu. Ieyasu was happy to employ Tenzen.

Munenori was never a man who lacked common sense or acted recklessly, but was, as Tenzen had imagined, highly principled and sensible. Tenzen as well was at a point where he had unshakeable confidence in himself, so he had this match against Munenori. Great minds think alike, so Tenzen and Munenori

73

became friends and supported each other in their devotion to protecting the Tokugawa Shogunate.

Distinguished Service at Hizaori Village

A major uproar occurred in the village of Hizaori, which lay on the outskirts of Edo, and it became a matter that increased the reputation of Tenzen. A rōnin named Onime, who was expert with the sword, forced his way into Hizaori Village and terrorized the place by murdering, robbing, assaulting women and girls, and eventually barricading himself in a farm house. The villagers were so terrified that none dared get close. Because there was no one around who could deal with this situation, the village chief sought an audience with the shogunate in Edo and begged for help.

"If you don't send Mikogami Tenzen, we will never be able to bring this violent swordsman under control. It is hoped that you will issue an order to Tenzen to put this criminal to death," he pleaded.

When Ieyasu heard this appeal, he decided to dispatch Tenzen to Hizaori and send Obata Kagenori along as an official inspector. [107] After they arrived together in Hizaori, they approached the front door of the house in which the swordsman had barricaded himself.

"I am Mikogami Tenzen. I have come here under orders to take the head of Onime. Either come out and fight like a man or we will come in and put you to death," he announced.

The swordsman, hearing Tenzen's challenge, replied: "I have been hearing of the reputation of Tenzen for quite some time. Now we meet. I have never been happier in my life. I'm coming out, so let's fight it out."

He came flying through the door. Onime stood around seven feet tall, and with his ferocious energy and outsized features looked much bigger because he was charging down from uphill. Onime held a three-foot long sword with a hilt wrapped in rattan high overhead and started to cut down toward Tenzen's head. Tenzen, realizing what was happening, pulled out his twenty-seven-and-a-half inch sword into a wakigamae stance, and then swept his sword upward under Onime's arms, slicing them off. Tenzen looked at the official inspector and asked if he should finish him off. When Obata gave the nod of approval, he beheaded him. Tenzen and Kanbei returned to Edo, where Kanbei made a detailed report to Ieyasu. Ieyasu rewarded Tenzen with a major promotion, elevating him to the rank of hatamoto and granting him a fief of 300 koku.[108]

Tenzen followed the decree of the shogun, restoring law and order to the village after ridding the place of a vicious criminal, and because he showed himself to be a true warrior, he became quite famous and earned the respect and gratitude of all people. When explaining what sword techniques he used that day to his students, he said, "The sword of *jun* (順) should cut off the enemy's arms, and the sword of *gyaku* (逆) should cut off his head. This is the best way to handle an enemy who comes on strong."

When Tenzen lopped off Onime's arms, the sword still in Onime's hands made contact with the headband he had been wearing on his forehead, slicing it. Taking that as a bad omen, he extended the length of Ittō-ryū's sword one half inch, making it twenty-eight inches[109] long. Tenzen always warned his students about this, however, and taught them the lessons of: *Judging distance is in the mind and not in the length of the sword; the long and short are the same;*[110] and the secret of the *No-sword.*[111]

The Seven Spears of Ueda and
the Stab of Ittō-ryū

Tokugawa Ieyasu took advantage of Toyotomi Hideyori's youth after the death of his father Hideyoshi and established himself in Edo after bringing the eight domains of the Kanto region under his control. Eager to make a move, he was thoroughly focused on determining the best opportunity to pounce, shoring up public support, solidifying his own faction, recruiting allies, and mustering his warriors. Tenzen was given an important position and assigned to serve under the banner of Ieyasu's son Hidetada.

The balance of power within Japan would soon be in flux and start shifting away from the Toyotomi, and it was far from certain whether it would go to Tokugawa, tilt toward Maeda Toshiie, or would fall to Ishida Mitsunari. At this point in time, a major historical sorting out would take place at Sekigahara, and it would be at this critical juncture where Japan's future would be decided. Hidetada received his orders from Ieyasu to open a second front around Sekigahara, and on August 24, 1600 departed Utsunomiya toward Shinano with 38,000 troops under his command. From the town of Komoro, Hidetada headed toward Ueda[112] Castle and attacked Sanada Yukimura and Sanada Masayuki, both of whom had sided with the Western Army and were defending the castle, but the Sanada forces put up a solid defense and the castle wouldn't fall easily. Hidetada's army fought hard but the siege dragged on until September 7th.

On that day, Hidetada's opening move was to deploy his forces into the rice fields around the castle [where they cut down the rice] and managed to restrain themselves from attacking. But at a strategic moment, a powerful force threw open the castle gates and sallied forth in the attack, slamming into Hidetada's army. That's when Tokugawa's valiant hatamotos Mikogami Tenzen, Toda Hanbei,[113] Tsuji Tarōnosuke,[114] Asakura Zōjūrō,[115] Nakayama

Sukerokurō, [116] Saito Kyuemon, [117] and Ota Kanshiro [118] distinguished themselves above all others by beating back the attack, fighting side-by-side. Due to this feat of arms, they became known throughout the Kanto region as the "Seven Spears[119] of Ueda" or "Seven Spears of Karita." [120] During this battle, Yoda Hyōbu, [121] Yamamoto Seiemon, [122] and Saito Sadayu [123] among others from the Sanada side, threw caution to the wind and fought furiously. In the skirmish, Mikogami Tenzen dealt a blow to the head of Yoda Hyōbu. Tsuji Tarōnosuke followed up with a cut of his own.

Yamamoto Seiemon saw this, hoisted the mortally wounded Hyōbu over his shoulder, and retreated back into the castle. Tenzen fought like a wild tiger and cut, stabbed, and slashed the bellies of a countless number of brave enemy warriors who came at him from all sides. The next day, the question of who cut Yoda Hyōbu first, Tenzen or Tarōnosuke, was an unresolved point taken up during an official review of the meritorious deeds performed in the previous day's battle. Tenzen said that he slashed at his opponent's face because he wasn't wearing a cheek guard[124] under his vermillion helmet, as opposed to Tarōnosuke, who insisted that Yoda was wearing a vermillion helmet with cheek guards covering his face and that it was he who cut him. To resolve this discrepancy, Makino Hiroshige sent some retainers disguised as horse buyers around Ueda Castle where they happened to meet Yamamoto Seiemon and asked him his thoughts on the incident.

"Yoda Hyōbu was wearing a vermillion helmet without cheek guards. His face was slashed and he was covered in blood, so the guy who looked at him later probably thought he was wearing vermillion cheek guards. The person who says he wasn't wearing any face protection is most definitely the one who cut him first," Seiemon recalled. His comments made it clear that it was Tenzen who made the first cut.

When Tenzen was asked why he failed to bring back any heads of his enemies, he answered that he fought to fulfill his duty and had no thought of earning personal glory. That's why he didn't bring back a single severed head. "But I stabbed and slashed into the bellies of many strong enemy warriors, slaying them. If you doubt me, you should examine the bodies left on the battlefield and see for yourselves," he clarified.

An inspector went to the battlefield, examined the bodies closely, and saw that it was exactly as Tenzen had described. He also recognized that shameless samurai stole Tenzen's valor by cutting off the heads of high-ranking warriors that had been stabbed to death in the field by Tenzen. Due to this investigation, word spread of Tenzen's selfless-service and the fearsomeness of Ittō-ryū's stabbing techniques, and he earned tremendous respect from all around him. And when Hidetada heard this, he lauded his noble spirit and superior martial skills and increased his responsibilities even more. From the time Hidetada started in Komoro to when he returned to Edo, Tenzen marched with Hidetada's army from beginning to end.

Tenzen's Duel with Yamagami Daizō Renaming Himself Ono Jirōemon Tadaaki

Sekigahara delivered a huge victory to the Tokugawa, power and influence shifted back to Edo, and feudal lords throughout the land bowed to its authority. The mansions of these regional lords suddenly began to pop up all over Edo as they competed against each other in their splendor. People from all walks of life crowded the streets, prosperity returned, and warriors from the more than sixty provinces gathered there. During this period, an unrivaled swordsman named Yamagami Daizō rode into town. Famed for his extraordinary skills in kenjutsu, he beat all who challenged him and the capital held him in awe. The Bakufu got wind of this. By the Shogun's decree, Tenzen was ordered to engage Daizō in mortal combat. An area in the riding grounds in front of Edo Castle's Ōtemon gate was roped off and guards posted, and it was decided that this major bout would occur there in full view. Talk of this reverberated throughout Edo.

In this much-anticipated match, Daizō haughtily strode into the arena, while Tenzen comported himself with quiet dignity. At the signal, they both unsheathed their swords and faced off. For a short while, Daizō glared at Tenzen, sizing him up, and then hurled himself across the gap separating them, trying to cut down on the top of Tenzen's head. Tenzen, standing composed and seeing this attack in the nick of time, did a *deba* version of kiriotoshi, and with a clash of the swords, stabbed toward Daizō's throat. Daizō, surprised by the danger at his neck, immediately jumped back out of the way. Both sides closed in again to striking range. Daizō, not able to withstand the piercing energy[125] coming out of Tenzen's attacking seigan posture, fully committed himself and took a giant step toward Tenzen to cleave his head in two. Using the *iriba* version of kiriotoshi, Tenzen walked right under Daizō's blade and cut clean through his head to his jaw line, putting a decisive end to the contest. The dignified demeanor, dauntless courage, and miraculous skill of Tenzen became even more famous throughout the land. Tenzen, especially pleased that he had gained Hidetada's confidence, changed his name from *Yoshiaki* to *Tadaaki* after he was bestowed the character *tada* (忠) from Hidetada himself. Tenzen also changed his surname from *Mikogami* to *Ono*, which he took from his maternal grandfather. From that point onward he decided to call himself Ono Jirōemon Tadaaki.

79

Tadaaki's Special Tactics to Deal with Multiple Attackers

Word of Ono Jirōemon Tadaaki's unparalleled military exploits spread throughout Japan and he was swarmed by those who, wanting that kind of fame, appealed for "lessons." There were also fellows who envied his success and wanted to bring him down. One time he responded to an invitation from Setoguchi Bizen, a sword master from the Satsuma Domain who founded [a branch of] Jigen-ryū. After Tadaaki reached his mansion, went inside, and was being escorted into an inner parlor, he entered an area with a wooden floor about 350 square-feet, where about twenty burly warriors were waiting. When Tadaaki attempted to pass, they pulled their swords, surrounded him from wall to wall, and started to attack. Tadaaki was ready for this and dodged and weaved in all directions, quickly cutting down eight of his attackers and inflicting mortal wounds on three others. The rest who saw this scattered in fear. When Tadaaki went further inside, toward the back of the mansion, he came across a man wearing a red kimono top with wide sleeves[126] and whose hair was done up in the samurai style. When the man threw down both of his swords still in their scabbards, prostrated himself until his forehead banged on the floor, and apologized by saying, "Your skill is just like a god's. There is no way we can equal it," Tadaaki spared him, and immediately left the residence.

As he departed the area, he passed through a densely forested mountain when a dozen or so enemies emerged from the shadows and started to attack him with swords. Tadaaki cut down six of them on the spot and inflicted mortal wounds on five others when another guy appeared brandishing a nine-foot-long *kama-yari*[127] type of spear. When his spear tip pierced Tadaaki's right sleeve and got tangled up, Tadaaki took it away. Jumping forward, he cut the man from between his eyes to below his breast using a typical kesa-giri cut. The rest all shrunk back and scattered to the four winds. Tadaaki incorporated how he used the sword in these encounters into the Hon Mokuroku Scroll [128] as the lesson of *Dealing with Whatever Comes*.[129]

Tadaaki's fame grew even greater and he received an invitation from Lord Shimazu, the chief of the Satsuma Domain. "My vassals have been eagerly asking for a test of skills as part of their warrior training, so I would be grateful if you could come visit," he asked.

Tadaaki thought that if he were to go to the powerful Shimazu clan and beat them, in all likelihood he would be jumped by a mob and never get away alive. He privately explained this to a younger cousin and asked him to inform his family in the event he didn't come back. Because he was committed to attend a duel related to another issue, his cousin wasn't able to go with him, but wished him well. When Tadaaki went to the Shimazu residence, Lord Shimazu sent out his four best swordsmen.

When Tadaaki said, "This is a valuable opportunity, so I will take on all four at once. Come and give it a go," all four jumped up in a fit of anger and started to attack from all directions. They all fought Tadaaki but were completely crushed.

Tadaaki immediately struck them down, *whack-whack-whack-whack*. The warriors who had been watching from the sidelines gritted their teeth and started reaching toward the handles of their short swords. At that point, Lord Shimazu stood up, retired to a sitting room, and motioned for Tadaaki to join him. When Tadaaki followed, the daimyo sent his retainers out, locked the door behind them, and said he wanted his own match with Tadaaki, but when he stood and faced him, he gave up for no reason and pledged to be Tadaaki's loyal student. He unlocked the door and called for his retainers.

"I have just become a student of Mr. Ono. You should all do the same and practice with him," he announced.

Tadaaki was able to return home without incident. Sometime later, Lord Shimazu confided to Tadaaki: "The retainers of mine who watched in agony as four of my people were defeated all reached for their short swords when they saw this. If, on top of this, they had seen me lose, I suspected they all would have tried to cut you down without a second thought, so I locked the door so that they wouldn't be able to get in."

There was a time when Tadaaki, at the request of and with permission from Yagyū Tajima-no-Kami Munenori, accepted a match against several of Munenori's top students at the same time. Tadaaki faced Munenori's three strongest disciples: Kimura Sukekurō, Murata Yozō, and Idebuchi Heihachi, who all went at him at the same time. As they attacked, Tadaaki stepped in under Sukekurō's downward-slicing cut and immediately snatched his sword away, disarming him. With this sword, he held down both hands of Yozō, who was coming in from the left. At that instant, Heihachi, who was to his right rear, raised his sword in jōdan and started to cut toward Tadaaki, but Tadaaki ducked under it and slipped out and around to Yozō's rear while Heihachi's sword came crashing down on Yozō's head, knocking him out cold onto his rear end. These students of Yagyū commented that trying to fight Tadaaki was just like cutting water or like trying to grab air. Moreover, when they hit his sword, theirs just bounced off and they couldn't keep hold of it.

This is what Tadaaki taught regarding how to deal with multiple attackers:[130]

> No matter how many hundreds of enemies there are who approach, when they come close to cut, they approach from eight directions, so they really only add up to eight people. And of these eight, some will be close and others far, and some will get in close and back away quickly and others slowly. Out of these, you should cut down your

enemies one-by-one starting with the one who comes within two feet and raises his sword to strike. In this way, a multitude of people will be one person. It's also easy for a crowd of people to fall over each other in confusion whey they attack, but when you are by yourself, you can be calm and collected. When facing multiple opponents, you shouldn't just rush into the fray. You should draw them in close to you and then cut them down. When your opponent takes ten steps [toward you], take three toward him and then wheel around to the left, right, front, or rear. If you are surprised by multiple opponents and they sap your energy, you will become mentally and physically exhausted and your technique will fall apart. You should perform this cutting down of your enemies one-after-the-other in a never-ending cycle with a clear and focused mind.[131]

Admonishing those Who Commercialized the Martial Arts

Around this time there were those in Edo who made their living by starting schools, opening their rain shutters to allow passersby to view practice matches, and getting the crowds riled up. One day Tadaaki, accompanied by his attendants, happened to pass by one of these schools and stopped to observe from within the crowd. Not only because the way they were fencing was completely amateurish and violating all principles, but also because he seethed with anger that they were disgracing the martial arts by turning them into a commodity to be sold, he turned toward his attendants, and in an intentionally loud voice, mercilessly ridiculed the fencers every time they raised their swords to strike. The swordsmen inside were infuriated when they heard this, halted their practice, and shouted back: "I don't know what kind of gentleman you are, but if I just let what you said pass unchallenged, I won't have a school tomorrow. Since you say our skills are so shameful, come forward and we will have a fair fight!" The crowd around Tadaaki all turned toward him thinking, *it's on now!* Without hesitation, Tadaaki stepped up onto the wooden floor of the dojo and, without touching the swords on his waist, took out a *hananeji*[132] used for horses instead and faced his challenger. Tadaaki smashed through the sword tip of the fencer, who was holding his sword in a showy stance, and then bounded forward through the gap, whacking him on the bridge of his nose. Blood gushed out as he fell flat on his back, seeing stars. The crowd around him thought, *a brawl!* let out a scream, and surged toward the exits all at once. Just then a different teacher who was there came forward, saying: "Needless to say, we shouldn't take the match that just happened too seriously. We will look after the person you just defeated today, but tomorrow, after we clean up this place, I want you to come back so you can have another bout, this time with me."

"I accept," Tadaaki said, and with that, went home.

The next day Tadaaki returned to check out the situation and saw that the outside of the dojo had changed from the day before. Onlookers were refused entry and only one of the side doors was open. Tadaaki turned to his attendant and wondered aloud: "Is he hiding behind the door waiting to attack? That isn't behavior befitting a warrior – the shameless coward! I really need to teach this guy a lesson." At that, Tadaaki flung himself through the open door like a bolt of lightning. But someone had spread oil on the wooden floor to make it slippery and there was nothing to keep his momentum from carrying him forward. Tadaaki's feet came out from under him and he fell straight onto his back.

Thinking everything was going according to plan, his challenger, who was lying in wait inside with his sword raised high overhead, brought his blade straight down to cleave Tadaaki in two as if he were executing a prisoner. While Tadaaki was falling, he whipped out his sword, known as the *Nabetsuri*[133], from his waist and instantly cut the guy in two. He then got up, re-sheathed his weapon, and walked out of the dojo as if nothing had happened. No one who heard of Tadaaki's actions failed to admire his willingness to step up and risk his life for the sake of the Way by getting rid of the evil that besmirched the martial arts or his exquisite sword skills that enabled him to fluidly respond to the sudden danger he faced. After word spread of this incident, those in Edo who were making money off the martial arts by commercializing them disappeared into the shadows and the Way of the Sword was held in even higher esteem.

The Indomitable Tadaaki

Tadaaki was a man of impeccable integrity and unequaled martial skill. A certain daimyo invited him to his domain, saying: "My retainers would like to see your skills. Can you come give us a demonstration?"

Tadaaki got a serious look on his face. "It sounds like they want a match. Don't hesitate to bring someone out. I will be their opponent," he replied.

When the match started sometime later, Tadaaki turned his wooden sword around so it was backwards and faced his opponent. "Well, isn't this an unnecessary request made on a whim? It would be a shame for you to get injured," he said while getting ready. His opponent, ruffled by these remarks, took up a seigan posture and glared at him while edging closer. Tadaaki hit his opponent's sword upward from below and sent it flying. He then brought his sword back around from above and hammered it down on both arms of his opponent. "Did you see that?" he asked, stepping back. "Your arms must be broken," he calmly stated. His opponent passed out for a short while and was hauled away for medical help by a page boy. Sure enough, he couldn't use his arms after he came to.

Tadaaki taught the kumitachi to his students every day while continuing to refine his own abilities. When he happened upon a worthy rival, he would happily accept a match using whatever weapon he had at hand: sharpened swords, blunted swords, wooden training swords, or whatever else was around. In his later years, because there was no one who could stand against him, he made a striking post the size and shape of a human body, woke up early every morning, and practiced striking and stabbing it thousands of times with a large wooden sword. To the very end, he developed tremendous physical strength and skill in striking and stabbing, and never stopped in his efforts to unite his mind, ki, and physical abilities.[134]

Tadaaki's Reputation and Daring

As a martial arts teacher, Tadaaki was an extremely strict taskmaster, even toward the Shogun, and never toadied up to him by going easy on him.[135] This was due to his devotion to the Way and it reflected how he truly felt toward his superior. One day Hidetada was talking about sword techniques and Tadaaki, who heard him pushing some half-baked idea he'd come up with, was worried about Hidetada's swelled head. Braving the Shogun's displeasure, Tadaaki said that the debate over this or that theory of fighting would never be settled unless swords were drawn. He warned that empty talk about the martial arts was the same as "swimming on dry land," and after he explained the real meaning of Ittō-ryū's *A Thousand Leagues is Decided by One Cut*,[136] Hidetada got the point.

Tadaaki was entrusted with the important job of official instructor of Ittō-ryū to the shogunate and his duties spanned from the second shogun, Hidetada, to the third, Iemitsu. For quite some time, Iemitsu had been thinking he would like to test the martial skills and temperament of both the renowned Ono Jirōemon Tadaaki and Yagyu Tajima-no-Kami Munenori. He sent a messenger to both, summoning them to hurry to the castle. He ordered a courtier to lay in ambush along a passageway leading into the castle and attack them without warning with a wooden sword when they passed by. Munenori approached first and easily brushed aside the attack with his folding fan. He then proceeded into the castle. Tadaaki, unaware of this and arriving a bit later, felt an evil presence, somehow sensed it was a trap, and avoided it entirely by entering through a different passageway, preventing the attack from taking place. This keen intuition was something he had learned from Ittōsai, and he was highly commended for his acumen and the dignified way he handled this test.

Even toward Iemitsu, Tadaaki maintained his exacting standards of training. But since he didn't take it upon himself to curry favor with Iemitsu, he would get under Iemitsu's skin for the slightest offense, get reprimanded, and be confined under house arrest. During one of these periods, Iemitsu went hunting in Itabashi but there was a violent bandit there murdering, ravaging houses, rampaging throughout the area, and terrorizing townsfolk. People were afraid to get too close. Upon hearing this, Iemitsu ordered Tadaaki to put the brigand to death. Unfortunately, Tadaaki was sick in bed when he heard the order and his students tried to hold him back, worried about his health, but he would have none of it. Rising from his sickbed, he eventually proceeded to Itabashi by palanquin and got out when he arrived at the house where the bandit was holed up. He put the criminal to death on the spot with one cut of his sword. Iemitsu, hearing that Tadaaki accomplished his mission at the risk of his own health, heaped praises upon him and released him from his confinement.

After Tadaaki was released and reported for duty, Iemitsu secretly suspected that he had neglected his training the entire time he was under arrest, while he himself had been practicing hard day and night, so he devised a plan to test his own skills against Tadaaki. He spread out a carpet in an area of the floor and placed two wooden swords tip-to-tip in the middle of it.

"The time has come for me to face Jirōemon right here," the Shogun decreed.

Tadaaki bowed down and placed his hands on the edge of the carpet when Iemitsu suddenly grabbed his sword and raised it high overhead and started to strike with a loud *Yah!* Tadaaki yanked the edge of the carpet he was holding, taking Iemitsu's feet out from under him and sending him backward with a thud. That's how Tadaaki taught Iemitsu the importance of observing his opponent.[137]

Tadaaki Finalizes Ittō-ryū

From the time he was a young man, Ono Jirōemon Tadaaki accompanied Itō Ittōsai, faithfully followed his teachings, and trained himself doggedly. He pushed himself, overcame adversity, developed his mind, and devised special sword techniques. He learned from his teacher, sharpened his skills against his contemporaries, trained his students, tested and toughened himself in contests with famous warriors from other schools, and in particular, never neglected his daily routine of striking a wooden post thousands of times a day with a wooden sword. Even at times when he was on duty at his government post, he would always wake up early and strike the post thousands of times while others were still in bed. Aside from his unparalleled genius, he trained day and night, and later, even though he reached brilliant achievements in war and was lauded for his masterly technique, his dedication never wavered and he finally perfected Ittō-ryū. As part of that process, he came up with the ways to practice and teach the kumitachi, and compiled the Odachi, Kodachi, Aikodachi, Sanjū, Habiki, Hosshatō, Goten, Taryū Katchi-no-Tachi, Tsumesa Battō, and other kata into the broad curriculum of Ittō-ryū. He distributed both principles of the sword and principles of the mind into each of the techniques in these kata, and taught the concept of the unassailable *The Sword and Mind are as One*.[138] Moreover, he codified these principles within the *Jūnikajo, Kanajisho, Hon,* and *Wari* scrolls, and established the fundamental principles of the Way of the Sword based on his outlook on the cosmos, humanity, and society.

After Tadaaki finished this great accomplishment, he shut himself up in the Sōsenji Temple of Shiba in Edo[139] and had many discussions with well-known priests renowned for their encyclopedic knowledge of morals and ethics. He deeply explored, parsing every word and phrase, the corpus of Japanese and Chinese studies, which form the essence of Japanese martial arts, exhausted every principle laid out within them, refined and formalized them, and presented them to Tokugawa Ieyasu and Hidetada for their review. Aside from teaching various daimyo, he also welcomed many other disciples and passed on to them the brilliant philosophy of the *Non-Ultimate of the Circle of the One Sword*[140] created by the founder, Itō Ittōsai Kagehisa, unstoppable techniques for the warrior, and the noble and ethical path a master should travel. Through Ittō-ryū, he was revered as a world-renowned teacher and put in place these martial virtues for future generations. After earning a name for himself by accomplishing all this, he fell ill and passed away in Edo on November 7, 1628. Upon his death he was given the Buddhist name of Seiganin Dono Meitatsu Daikyoshi.[141] His grave is on the mountain behind the

Eikoji Temple in Sōshū, Inba-gun, Narita Town. A wooden statue of him is enshrined in the temple.

Gravestones of Ono Tadaaki and his son.

Endnotes to Chapter Three

91 Two shaku, eight sun.

92 One shaku, five sun, five bu.

93 *Musha shugyō* (武者修業)

94 *Zuishin* (随身)

95 *Yuijuichinin no hō* (唯授一人の法)

96 The term *kiai* (気合) has no formal definition, but in this context refers to neutralizing an opponent through using one's *ki* (気), or intrinsic energy,

97 *Zenki matsu* (善鬼松)

98 *Buke* (武家)

99 This was the inn district within Kanda.

100 Nicknamed the "Bloody Spear."

101 *Hatamoto* (旗本); also referred to as *bannermen*.

102 *Chūdachi* (中太刀)

103 Yagyu Tajima-no-Kami Munenori (柳生但馬の神宗矩) was the founder of the Edo branch of the Yagyū Shinkage-ryū school of swordsmanship.

104*Daisho* (大小)

105A sleeveless ceremonial robe worn by samurai.

106 *Kagowaki* (籠脇)

107 *Kenshiyaku* (検使役)

108 Retainers were paid in rice in units of *koku*. One koku was considered enough rice to feed one man for an entire year. So, theoretically at least, Tadaaki should have been able to keep a household and enough manpower to field three hundred people if called upon.

109 Two shaku, three sun, five bu.

110 *Chōtan Ichimi* (長短一味)

111 *Mutō no Kokoroe* (無刀の心得)

112 The original text says "Shimada" (下田), however, the historical facts and context in the following paragraphs suggest Shimada is a typographical mistake.

113 Toda Hanbei (戸田半兵)

114 Tsuji Tarōnosuke (辻太郎助)

115 Asakura Zōjūrō (朝倉臓十郎)

[116] Nakayama Sukerokurō (中山助六郎)

[117] Saito Kyuemon (齋藤久衛門)

[118] Ota Kanshiro (太田勘四郎)

[119] The term *spears* was an appellation denoting bravery and was given to those who most distinguished themselves in battle. It doesn't necessarily mean actual spears were involved in the fighting.

[120] *Karita* (苅田) can be loosely translated as *harvest*. This appellation refers to the fact that Hidetada's army was harvesting rice around the castle when they were attacked.

[121] Yoda Hyōbu (依田兵部)

[122] Yamamoto Seiemon (山本清右衛門)

[123] Saito Sadayu (齋藤左太夫)

[124] *Hodate* (頬盾)

[125] *Shinei no ki* (真鋭の気)

[126] *Hirosode* (比呂袖)

[127] *Kama-yari* (鎌鑓); a spear tip with a horizontal blade at the base that allows the wielder to entangle an opponent's clothing.

[128] *Honmokuroku* (本目録)

[129] *Happō Bunshin* (八方分身)

[130] *Tateki no kurai* (多勢の位)

[131] *Shinki* (心気)

[132] *Hananeji* (鼻捻): a tool to control horses, similar to a riding crop.

[133] *Nabetsuri* (鍋釣)

[134] *Shinkiryoku icchi* (心気力一致)

[135] The text refers to *tonosama keiko*, which means dilettantish training or practice.

[136] *Banri ittō ni kessu* (万里一刀に決る)

[137] *Futatsu no Metsuke* (二之目付)

[138] *Kenshin ichinyo* (剣心一如)

[139] Sōsenji Temple of Shiba in Edo (柴葉の宗泉寺)

[140] *Ittō Ensō Mukyoku* (一刀円相無極); this term has a deep philosophical meaning. *Ittō* refers to One Sword; *ensō* refers to the infinite and boundless; and *mukyoku* refers to the Ultimate of Non-being in Chinese philosophy.

[141] *Seiganin Dono Meitatsu Daikyoshi* (清岸院殿明達大居士)

CHAPTER FOUR

Record of Itō-ryū's Main Line, Branches, and Factions

Itō Ittōsai Kagehisa: Founder of Itō-ryū. Refer to Chapter Two, *Life of Itō Ittōsai Kagehisa, Founder of Itō-ryū* of this book.

Ono Jirōemon Tadaaki: Succeeded Ittōsai as the heir of the main line of Itō-ryū after learning directly from him; named this legitimate line of Itō-ryū the *Ono-ha* [Ono faction] to distinguish it from other factions and branches. Refer to Chapter Three, *Life of Ono Jirōemon Tadaaki* of this book.

Ono Jirōemon Tadaaki's eldest son died prematurely.

> **Itō Tenzen Tadanari:** Tadaaki's second son. Born in 1602 as Mikogami Tenzen Tadanari but later changed his surname to Itō. He was called both *Chūya* (忠弥) and *Tadanari* (忠成). Learned Itō-ryū from his father, Tadaaki, but was expelled from his father's household and created a new faction named Chūya-ha Itō-ryū (忠也派一刀流).[142]

Itō Tadao: Originally known as Kamei Heiemon. Adopted by Tadanari as a son; succeeded Tadanari as the head of Chūya-ha Ittō-ryū.

Itō Heisuke: Eldest son of Heiemon; changed the spelling of his name from Itō (伊藤) to Itō (井藤); succeeded Itō Tadao as head of Chūya-ha Ittō-ryū.

Negoro Yakurō Shigeaki: Third son of Heiemon; learned Ittō-ryū from his father; founded Tenshin Dokumyō-ryū (天 心 独 名 流). Served Niwa Nagatsugu, Lord of the Nihonmatsu Domain.

Ono Jirōemon Tadatsune: Tadaaki's third son; first named Tadakatsu. Learned the system of Ittō-ryū from his father; succeeded him as sōke; and, upon succession, took the name *Jirōemon*. Thereafter, all of those who succeeded as the legitimate heir of Ittō-ryū took the name *Jirōemon* as part of the succession process. In addition to Shogun Tokugawa Iemitsu, Tadatsune taught many other students. He was banished to Kazusa Province for a short while but was later called back to Edo. Tadatsune's skills were equal to the masterful techniques of his father, and he grasped the absolute truth of Ittō-ryū's secret Musōken. He added the four moves of Deba, Iriba, Yorimi, and Koshimi to the fifty moves of the Odachi kata of Ittō-ryū's kumitachi; he died at the age of fifty-eight on November 6, 1665.

Kaji Shinemon Masanao: Student of Tadatsune while he was still known as Tadakatsu; founded the Kaji-ha Ittō-ryū (梶 派 一 刀 流). Became a member of the Tokugawa Household Guard.[143]

Matsumoto Ko-Okinokami:[144] Student of Tadatsune.

Mizoguchi Hanemon: Member of the shogun's marine guard;[145] student of Tadatsune.

Sakabe Magashiro: Palace guard;[146] student of Tadatsune.

Okada Awaji: Shogunal bodyguard; [147] student of Tadatsune.

Tadatsune trained roughly 4,200 students.

Ono Jirōemon Tadao: Tadaaki's fourth son; adopted by Tadatsune. An alternative explanation is that he was one of Tadaaki's students. Learned and mastered the entire system of Ittō-ryū from Tadatsune and then worked as the official instructor to the shoguns Ietsuna, Tsunayoshi, and Ienobu. Added a total of six additional moves to the Odachi kata: three comprising Aiba and three comprising Hariaiba, which completed the kumitachi of Ittō-ryū. Died December 29, 1712, at the age of 73.

Tsugaru Nobumasa: Fourth-generation Lord of the Tsugaru Domain; mastered the secrets of Ittō-ryū from Tadao and was noted for his accomplishments in both the literary and martial arts.

Mizuno Kenmotsu, Amano Denshiro, Arita Jueimon, Sakai Ukyo-no-Suke, Hirano Kyuzaemon, Saegusa Noto-no-Kami, and Sakai Udayu were among the 3,414 students Tadao trained (as of February 7, 1710).

Ono Jirōemon Tadakazu: Originally named Okabe Sukekurō; adopted by Tadao; changed his name to Tadakazu; learned Ittō-ryū from Tadao and mastered the system; died May 17, 1738.

Aside from teaching the Tokugawa Shogunate, Tadakazu had many other students. He didn't pass on the legitimate line of Ittō-ryū to his son but transmitted the full system to Tsugaru Tosa-no-Kami Nobuhisa. Tadakazu died in 1738.

Tsugaru Tosa-no-Kami Nobuhisa: Fifth-generation lord of the Tsugaru Domain; mastered the inner secrets of Ittō-ryū from Tadao and inherited the system of Ittō-ryū as his sole successor. It was for this reason that the direct transmission of the main line of Ittō-ryū temporarily passed from the House of Ono to the House of Tsugaru.

Ono Jirōemon Tadahisa: Was going to inherit the main line of Ittō-ryū from Tsugaru Nobuhisa but died prematurely.

Ono Jirōemon Tadakata: His father, Tadahisa, died at a young age while Tadakata was still an infant so he wasn't able to learn Ittō-ryū from him. Lamenting that Ittō-ryū might tragically come to an end within the House of Ono, Tsugaru Nobuhisa came out of retirement in his old age and taught Ittō-ryū to Tadakata as he got older, passing on the entire system to him and enabling him to succeed as the head of the main line. Tadakata died October 16, 1749.

Ono Jirōemon Tadayoshi: Son of Tadakata; learned from his father and had many students. Died October 29, 1798.

Ono Jirōemon Tadataka: Son of Tadayoshi; learned Ittō-ryū from his father and succeeded him as the head of the mainline.

Ono Jirōemon Tadasada: Son of Tadataka; learned from his father; received the full inheritance of Ittō-ryū.

Ono Nario: Learned the system of Ittō-ryū from his father.

Nakanishi Chūta Tanesada: Student of Ono Jirōemon Tadakazu; opened an Ittō-ryū training hall in Edo and trained a large number of students. This school is now commonly referred to as the Nakanishi-ha Ittō-ryū.

Nakanishi Chūzō Tanetake: Succeeded Tanesada; devised face and chest protectors (modern day kendo protective gear) starting from 1763 and incorporated the bamboo practice sword, which laid the groundwork for modern competitive kendo.

Nakanishi Chūta Tsuguhiro: Succeeded Tanetake.

Nakanishi Chūbei Tsugumasa: Succeeded Tsuguhiro and had many students; produced such notables as Takayanagi Matashiro and Kakizaki Kensuke, among others.

> **Chiba Shūsaku:** Studied under both Tsuguhiro and Tanetake; created Hokushin Ittō-ryū (北辰一刀流).

> **Terada Muneari:** Studied under both Tsuguhiro and Tanetake; created Tenshin Ittō-ryū (天真一刀流).

> **Asari Yoshinobu:** Studied under both Tsuguhiro and Tanetake; taught their sons.

> **Asari Yoshiaki:** Studied Ittō-ryū under Tsuguhiro, Tanetake, and his father, Yoshinobu; developed exquisite skill.

Yamaoka Tesshū: Studied Ittō-ryū under Yoshiaki; created Mutō-ryū (無刀流).

Takano Mitsumasa: Studied under Tsugumasa and taught Tsugumasa's son Takano Kansei.[148] His son, Takano Sasaburō Tomimasa, was famous throughout the Meiji, Taisho, and Showa eras.

Yamaga Hachirōemon Takami: Fourth-generation Yamaga after Yamaga Sokō; received the inner-most secret documents[149] and license to operate a dojo from Ono Jirōemon Tadayoshi. He had many students, among them: Tsugaru Nobuyuki, Araki Sekiyaemon, Akamatsu Keizo, Saito Kumzo, Tateyama Iwajiro, Mitsuhashi Harunoshin, and Sudō Hanbei.

Sudō Hanbei Masatake[150]: Studied under Yamaga Takami. His students who were known as the "Four Emperors"[151] were: Wada Kenichiro, Matsui Shiro, Oka Kakuma, and Tsushima Kakuzō.

Sudō Hannomune Masayasu[152]: Studied under his father and developed exquisite skill.

Tsushima Kenpachi: Learned Ittō-ryū from his father, Kakuzō; mastered the secrets; and taught the children of Hirosaki at the Hokushindo Dojo.

Yamaga Jirosaku Takaatsu: Second son of Takami; learned Ittō-ryū from his father; received the secrets from Ono Jirōemon Tadataka; and became the Chief Instructor of Ittō-ryū to the Tsugaru Domain. Takaatsu's son Tomozō Takahisa studied under his father and succeeded him, and his son Morie Takayuki received the same from his father. Takayuki's adopted son, Motojiro Takatomo, also received the full transmission of the school.

Kakizaki Kensuke: Studied Ittō-ryū under Nakanishi Tsugumasa and mastered its secrets; received the full transmission from the House of Ono as well; served the Tsugaru Domain. Those of his students who excelled included: Sasamori Teiji, Ito Manzō, and Honda Kenichi.

Kakizaki Kensuke Junior: Studied under his father and made a name for himself through Ittō-ryū.

Nakahata Hidegoro: Studied Ittō-ryū under Kensuke Sr.; mastered its secrets; had many students who became famous throughout Japan. He was related to the Kakizaki family.

Sasamori Junzō: First learned Ittō-ryū under Tsushima Kenpachi; later received the secrets of the entire curriculum of the techniques of the kumitachi from Nakahata Hidegoro. Moreover, he was bestowed the secret documents[153] from Yamaga Takatomo, as well as the highest-level secrets passed on to only one heir from Tsugaru Nobuhisa, making him the successor of the mainline of Ittō-ryū. (Refer to the Foreword of this book.)

Endnotes to Chapter Four

[142] Also called Itō-ha Ittō-ryū (伊藤派一刀流) in some sources.

[143] *Ōbanshū* (大番衆)

[144] Matsumoto Ko-Okinokami (松本故隠岐守)

[145] *Ofunate* (御船手)

[146] *Ōgoban* (大御番)

[147] *Okosho* (御小姓)

[148] Takano Kansei (高野蕃正)

[149] *Ōhisho* (奥秘書)

[150] Sudō Hanbei Masatake (須藤半兵正万)

[151] *Shitennō* (四天王)

[152] Sudō Hannomune Masayasu (須藤半之極正安)

[153] *Hidensho* (秘伝書)

CHAPTER FIVE

Transmission of Ittō-ryū from the Ono to the Tsugaru

The story of how the legitimate line of Ittō-ryū passed between the House of Ono and the House of Tsugaru is described in detail below. During the Bakufu period, the foremost feudal domains that considered the martial arts to be important and the martial arts masters who aspired to elevate their status formed extremely close ties in various ways, and this case is a good example to show how the pedigree of a school of swordsmanship[154] was transferred between the master of one of these schools and a feudal lord.

Tsugaru Tosa-no-Kami Nobuhisa was a daimyo who devoted his energies to Ittō-ryū, mastered its secrets, and demonstrated real ability in it. While at the same time, even though Ono Sukekurō Tadakazu was the sōke of Ittō-ryū, because he was in a position to receive a stipend of nearly 800 koku as one of Tokugawa's hatamotos, there was never a doubt that once the system of Ittō-ryū was bestowed upon the House of Tsugaru, which had requested it, it would once again be passed back to an ancestor of the House of Ono. Below are the contents of the oath proffered by Ono Sukekurō when he bequeathed the system of Ittō-ryū to Tsugaru Tosa-no-Kami Nobuhisa. It's useful reference material that shows the exact circumstances surrounding his decision.

To: Lord Tsugaru Tosa-no-Kami

Preface to My Oath to the Gods

The Ittō-ryū school of strategy has continued for five generations, from Ittōsai down to me. Every word and every movement has, without exception, been preserved. However, I bear responsibility for preventing this tradition from being lost. This vow is different from most. I have a duty to preserve all the secret teachings and must therefore permit the teachings of this school. There should be no doubt that the above is wholly accurate and that the school is only transmitted to one disciple. Thus, I exchange this vow under the old way of doing things.

I offer the above statement aware of the consequences as outlined below.

Should I break the oath written in this document, I submit myself to the punishment of Bonten, Taishaku-ten, the Four Heavenly Kings, the gods of heaven and earth, great, medium, and small, of the more-than-sixty provinces of Japan, especially the two avatars of Izu and Hakone, the Bright Deity of Mishima, the Great Bodhisattva Hachiman, Tenman Daijizai Tenjin, and in particular the Great Protector Marishiten and the local deities who protect us.

March 11, 1718
Blood seal of Ono Sukekurō

The above provides proof of the bestowal of all of the secrets of Ittō-ryū from Ono Jirōemon Tadakazu, around the time he was called Sukekurō, to Tsugaru Tosa-no-kami Nobuhisa as the sole heir of the school. The contents of Nobuhisa's oath, addressed to Sukekurō in reply, is below:

To: Lord Ono Sukekurō

Preface to My Oath to the Gods

The secrets of the Ittō-ryū school of strategy have been handed down from the founding teacher, Ittōsai Kagehisa. This has been my earnest desire for a great number of years. I am overjoyed at receiving the transmission of this school. I will transmit the tenets of this school to Lord Iori, who shares your family name. Furthermore, the school will be transmitted to only one student. That is all. The tenets of this school will be guarded.

I offer the above statement aware of the consequences as outlined below.

(The written oath declaring his intentions before the gods is repeated in the original but has been omitted here for brevity.)

March 11, 1718
Tsugaru Tosa-no-kami

The original document transcribed above was sent from the House of Tsugaru to the House of Ono and a copy was preserved within the Tsugaru family as a duplicate record. Once Tsugaru Nobuhisa received the transmission of Ittō-ryū from Ono Sukekurō Tadakazu, he made a vow to pass the main line of Ittō-ryū back to Tadakazu's son Ono Iori at a later time. When that time came, Nobuhisa passed on the full transmission of Ittō-ryū to Iori, also known as Ono Jirōemon Tadahisa, as promised. The written oath Iori forwarded to Nobuhisa is transcribed below:

To: Lord Tsugaru Tosa-no-kami

Preface to my Oath to the Gods

I have heard and understood that I will receive the transmission from my father, Tadakazu Sukekurō. I wish his house the greatest prosperity. I do not believe I will be able to achieve the level of my forebears.

My venerable Lord has entrusted me to be the next inheritor of the Ittō-ryū school of strategy. This school has been handed down from my esteemed ancestor Ittōsai until the current fifth generation head, Sukekurō Tadakazu. I understand that each and every prescript of the school must be maintained without the slightest error.

I will not reveal the secrets of our family's school to other people. Further, I will use the teachings entrusted to me in the service of my lord. I hereby swear to abide by these commandments.

I offer the above statement aware of the consequences as outlined below.

(The written oath declaring his intentions before the gods is repeated in the original but has been omitted here for brevity.)

March 11, 1718
Blood seal of Ono Iori

As is made clear above, it was documented in writing that Ono Sukekurō Tadakazu's son, Iori Tadahisa, wouldn't inherit the system of Ittō-ryū from his father, Tadakazu, but would instead inherit it from Tsugaru Tosa-no-Kami Nobuhisa. It was in this way that the sixth-generation headmastership was transferred to Tsugaru Nobuhisa. But in a strange twist of fate, if Ittō-ryū hadn't been passed to the House of Tsugaru at this time, the legitimate line of Ittō-ryū probably would have died out and not been carried on within the House of Ono. This is because Iori passed away without receiving the full transmission of Ittō-ryū while his son, Tadakata, was still a child, and due to this tragic turn of events, the main line could have died out within the House of Ono without the techniques and lessons being passed on.

The reason that Tsugaru Nobuhisa was able to rescue the main line from extinction within the House of Ono after the untimely death of Ono Jirōemon Tadahisa, who was in line to become the seventh-generation sōke of the main line of Ittō-ryū directly transmitted from Itō Ittōsai, was because Tadakazu temporarily bestowed the legitimate line of Ittō-ryū to him.

Nobuhisa, who took the name Sakaeō[155] after abdicating his position as chief of the domain in his twilight years, was enjoying a comfortable retirement pursuing the paths of literary and martial arts, but came out of retirement to once again teach the main line of Ittō-ryū to Tadakata, son of the deceased Tadahisa. A

105

copy of the transmission documents detailing this proposal is below.

To: Lord Ono Jirōemon

Ittō-ryū Kenjutsu's *Book of Inner Secrets*

These are the secrets that have been handed down within our family by all previous heads of the school. My father, Tsugaru Nobumasa, compiled these techniques after long years of study. This is what you are receiving. Due to your father, Tadahisa, our two houses have maintained a deep relationship. Unfortunately, Tadahisa left this world too early and, therefore, the training necessary for you to receive the transmission of this school is incomplete. It would be a great shame if this school were to be lost. The transmission of the inner secrets can only go to one person. I cannot remain silent on this. I would also like to keep this confidential. I will teach you the essential elements, but I respectfully request that you do no pass this information to more than one person.

November, 1743
Tsugaru Sakaeō

The original letter above was sent to Ono Jirōemon Tadakata, and a duplicate, written by the hand of Tsugaru Sakeō himself, has been preserved within the Tsugaru household. The written oath declaring his intentions before the gods[156] that was forwarded to Sakaeō by Tadakata in response to the above is transcribed below:

Oath

Preface to My Oath to the Gods

My grandfather, Jirōemon Tadakazu, told me about receiving the transmission of the school, and I offer my wish for the prosperity of your house. My father, Sukekurō Tadahisa, became the inheritor of the school of Ittō-ryū. Unfortunately, he passed from this earth too soon and, regrettably, I was unable to receive the full transmission.

I will diligently guard, without exception, all the precepts set down by the five generations of the Ittō-ryū school, starting from the founder, Ittōsai, through my grandfather, Jirōemon Tadakazu.

With regard to the teachings of the school of Ittō-ryū, I understand that the complete teachings can only be passed on to one disciple. However, I will also ensure that what has been preserved will not be lost through carelessness. I will ensure that the tradition of this household is maintained and passed on properly according to tradition. The school must not be passed on to a person who is not qualified. I do hereby promise to abide strictly by these precepts.

I offer the above statement aware of the consequences as outlined below.

Should I break the oath written in this document, I submit myself to the punishment of Bonten, Taishaku-ten, the Four Heavenly Kings, the gods of heaven and earth, great, medium, and small, of the more-than-sixty provinces of

Japan, especially the two avatars of Izu and Hakone, the Bright Deity of Mishima, the Great Bodhisattva Hachiman, Tenman Daijizai Tenjin, and in particular the Great Protector Marishiten and the local deities who protect us.

Ono Jirōemon Tadakata
Blood Oath and stylized signature.

As the contents above show, the Ittō-ryū that was handed down directly from Itō Ittōsai Kagehisa was transmitted to Ono Jirōemon Tadakata from Tsugaru Nobuhisa intact and unchanged.

The writer, Kudo Shuzen Tazan,[157] wrote the following about Nobuhisa in Volume 92 of his history of the Tsugaru Domain: "[He] mastered the secrets of martial arts master Ono Jirōemon and handed down all to the House of Ono..." The secret documents of the main line of Ittō-ryū were passed to the author of this book through the successive generations of the heads of the House of Tsugaru, passing from Nobuhisa through Nobuaki, Nobuyasu, Nobuakira, Yasuchika, Nobuyuki, Yukitsugu, Tsuguakira, and Hidemaro to the present generation head, Yoshitaka.[158] In addition to this, Ittō-ryū was passed through the House of Ono from Tadakata through Tadayoshi, Tadataka, Tadasada, to Nario,[159] and moreover, from Yamaga Hachiroemon Takami, who was initiated into the secrets from Ono Tadayoshi, through Takaatsu, Takahisa, Takayuki, and Takatomo to the author of this book.

Endnotes to Chapter Five

[154] *Ryūgi* (流儀)

[155] Sakaeō (栄翁)

[156] *Batsubun* (罰文)

[157] Kudo Shuzen Tazan (工藤主膳他山)

[158] Yoshitaka's daughter Hanako married Prince Masahito of the Imperial Family, becoming Her Royal Highness, the Princess Hitachi.

[159] Nario (業雄)

CHAPTER SIX

The Sudden Rise of Ittō-ryū within the Tsugaru Domain

Tsugaru Nobumasa,[160] the fourth-generation Lord of Tsugaru, attained the highest-level secrets of Ittō-ryū after studying under Ono Jirōemon Tadao, and the fifth-generation lord, Tsugaru Nobuhisa,[161] likewise, was initiated into all of the mysteries of the school by Tadao. The daimyo of Tsugaru who came after Tadakazu also studied this school, so the warriors within this domain who were highly motivated vied against each other, throwing their hearts into refining their skills in Ittō-ryū. As a result, there was a sudden rise in the popularity of Ittō-ryū among these warriors, both those remaining at home in Tsugaru and those dispatched to Edo, and distinguished experts cropped up one after another.

Tsugaru Nobumasa revered Yamaga Sokō and tried to get him to move to Tsugaru as his teacher and advisor, but Sokō dispatched his adopted son Okinobu[162] there to teach the Yamaga-ryū school of military strategy[163] in his stead. Takami,[164] Okinobu's great-great-grandson, attained the highest levels of Ittō-ryū, received all of the secrets from Ono Jirōemon Tadayoshi,[165] and cultivated many students. His son Yamaga Takaatsu was particularly skilled in Ittō-ryū and stood unrivaled in his generation. Since then, succeeding generations of the Yamaga family served the Tsugaru Domain by teaching both Ittō-ryū and Yamaga-ryū to a number of students.

The ninth-generation Lord of Tsugaru, Yasuchika,[166] founded the Keikokan, the Hirosaki Domain's primary education and training academy, and allocated it an annual operating budget of ten-thousand koku a year. This school put a premium on teaching the military and literary arts, and especially emphasized Ittō-ryū in its curriculum. It promoted Yamada Ichigaku[167] as the head instructor, hired Yamada Yūzō[168] as an assistant, and added Takeda Yagaku[169] and Yamada Kichijiro[170] as adjunct teachers. After that, Ittō-ryū surged in popularity among the sons of the domain's retainers who studied in this school, peaking from the end of the Edo period to the beginning of the Meiji era.

Sudō Hanbei Masatake[171] learned Ittō-ryū from Yamaga Takami, distinguished himself among his fellow students, and attained its highest-level secrets. There were many devoted students who learned at the feet of Masatake, and when he was sixty years old, they had a portrait of him made with an inscription to honor him. What they presented to his son Masayasu[172] as a gift had the following written on it:

Homage to our Instructor of the Ittō-ryū School of Fencing, Sudō Hanbei

Contributing to the prolongation of the Ono Family Branch of the Ittō-ryū School of Gekiken Fencing.

Our Domain has from long ago been influenced by both Yamaga Takami and Yamaga Takaatsu. Through their instruction, our own teacher, Sudō, was able to teach us

112

about what he learned in other domains and the true meaning of spirit. Finally, he taught us the inner meanings of the lessons handed down by Nakanishi Sensei.

Our teacher held countless lessons for the samurai of our domain, though we may have been less than adept as pupils. We feel compelled to illustrate the warmth and gratitude that we feel for him. If it were possible by the laws of our domain, we would have had him as our teacher for the next hundred years. Such is our passion for our teacher. All that remains is for us to do our best to develop ourselves based upon the lessons he taught us and pass that learning and wisdom on to the next generation.

Sincerely,
The Students and Instructors
February 1852

The ages of master Sudō, Official Domain Instructor, and the "Four Emperors" as of 1851 were:
Sudō Masatake Sensei – sixty years old
Matsui Shiro – thirteen years old
Tsushima Kakuzō – eleven years old
Oka Kakuma – ten years old
Wada Kenichiro – twelve years old.

[Images of]: Sudō Masatake; Wada Kenichiro, Matsui Shiro, Oka Kakuma, Tsushima Kakuzō.

The "Four Emperors" who studied Ittō-ryū under Sudō Hanbei and their successors were well known for their mastery of the art, and they taught many children of the Tsugaru Domain's elite.

113

Kakizaki Kensuke Sr. [173] first studied under Nakanishi Tsugumasa, obtained an endorsement from the House of Ono later, and became an instructor of Ittō-ryū, serving Tsugaru Yukitsugu.[174] Among his disciples who excelled, aside from his son Kensuke Jr., were Sasamori Teiji,[175] Ichinohe Manzō,[176] Honda Kenichi,[177] and Nakahata Hidegorō.[178] In his later years, Takano Sasaburō [179] frequented Hirosaki and studied Ittō-ryū under Nakahata Hidegorō. Hidegorō lived in Hirosaki City until his death on July 8, 1928, at the age of eighty-two, enthusiastically looking after the sons of the city and teaching Ittō-ryū in the Too-Gijuku, as well as other schools and city dojos. He passed on to the author of this book the system of Ittō-ryū as well as his secret transmission documents,[180] which he always kept close to his chest.

Honda Kenichi first learned Ittō-ryū from Kakizaki Kensuke Sr., was sent by his domain elders to Edo, and diligently trained there for three years under Nakanishi Chūta[181] and Asari Yoshiaki.[182] After he obtained the inner secrets from them, he returned home to report what he learned. The Lord of Tsugaru gave Kenichi permission to open a new dojo and granted him all the land, resources, and construction funds he needed. Kenichi's teacher, Kakizaki Kensuke Sr., died, however, and his son, Kensuke Jr., wasn't able to attract students due to his young age. Because the Kakizaki Dojo started to falter, Kenichi abandoned the idea of building a new school for his own sake and instead invested all of his resources into revitalizing his former dojo to repay his debt of gratitude toward his beloved teacher. Because he helped out Kensuke Jr. and threw all his efforts into rebuilding the Kakizaki Dojo, everyone admired not just his exquisite skill but also his character and students from all over were drawn to him. The Kakizaki Dojo thrived and produced such notable expert swordsmen as Susukida, [183] Fukuda, [184] Takemura, [185] Kimura, [186] Ōta,[187] Kosugi,[188] and Higuchi.[189] Honda Yoichi,[190] who was Honda Kenichi's nephew and originally named Tokuzō, also learned Ittō-

114

ryū at this dojo starting from when he was around fifteen years old.

The letter below that Asari Yoshiaki forwarded to Honda Kenichi is a good document to show how Kenichi maintained close ties with Yoshiaki and worked hard to disseminate Ittō-ryū. It also shows a young Yamaoka Tetsutarō's[191] strong desire to start training in Ittō-ryū around the same time.

To: Master Sudō Hannomune [Masayasu]
　　Master Honda Kenichi

Though I take up my brush to write you this letter in spring, the winds are cold.

I trust all is well and peaceful with you and your household as that is the most precious thing. I would like to humbly ask your opinion on a matter and see if you are of the same mind as me.

Recently, I have not been able to observe the training that has been conducted at the place in question. The last I saw the kenjutsu and other training, it was more or less going as you would expect, proceeding robustly. I would like to again thank you sincerely for all the assistance you have provided. Thinking back to the days at the dojo in Tokyo, there seems to be about the same number of people attending daily training. And with many of the students approaching higher levels of enlightenment I feel that we are truly blessed. No doubt this will lead to greater and greater things for Ittō-ryū.

There is an application from Yamaoka. When he arrives, he should join the school in the customary manner. Though I am aging and losing some of my ability, I would very much like to attend training when he arrives. I will leave training up to whomever is in charge at the time, even when I am in attendance. Yamaoka requests, if at all possible, to train with both of you when it is convenient. He has just left from Tokyo and is very interested in crossing swords after a long break due to his travels. No doubt, having a new person at the dojo will inspire the other students and improve training. I apologize for causing you to have to make preparations in a rush for this person arriving from Tokyo. Though he is starting in the middle of the year, Yamaoka will pay the entrance fee as usual. Below is his statement regarding joining the school and his understanding of the preparations required:

> *Here is my humble introduction. I served the Arisugawa no Miya.*
>
> *Though the Lord will soon be sixty-three years old, he is in robust health. Moreover, the hundredth anniversary of the birth of Nakanishi Chūzō Tanetake is approaching on June 13th and I would like to participate in the memorial.*
>
> *Though there may be things I am neglecting to say, I am in the midst of my preparations to depart from Tokyo and do hereby deliver my intention to enter your dojo.*

I apologize for any trouble you might be having and wish you the best of health.

February 15
Asari Matashichirō Yoshiaki

The Meiji Restoration rolled around, the directive banning feudal domains and replacing them with prefectures was promulgated, and the order banning the wearing of swords was issued in 1876. The Way of the Sword slipped into decline but interested parties who enjoyed doing the martial arts built schools in the four corners of Hirosaki City – *Hokushindo, Meijikan, Jōyōkai,* and the *Yōmeikan* – where they practiced all of the various schools and factions of martial arts, not just Ittō-ryū. The former official instructors of the feudal domains competed from within these schools to attract the best students. On the occasion to submit these martial arts for imperial review at Hirosaki City's Fushimi Grand Shrine on June 4, 1874, Ittō-ryū was the first to demonstrate. Honda Kenichi, serving as Uchikata, and Osanai Tatsumaro,[192] serving as Shikata, both showed consummate skill in demonstrating the secret Habiki kata. In this same demonstration, Tazawa Kumekichi[193] stood as Uchikata against Sudō Kanichirō[194] and Andō Taiichi [195] and put on a wonderful performance demonstrating Ittō-ryū's kumitachi. Despite our elders who enjoyed these types of old-style martial arts passing away from the Meiji through the Taisho to the Showa eras, in Hirosaki City, starting with the rebirth of the Too-Gijuku from the Keikokan, the former Tsugaru Domain training academy, various public schools, dojo, police precincts, Butokukai branches, military units, and others, put a premium on the Way of the Sword as evidenced, in particular, by the establishment of the Gokokukan Dojo and the formation of the Aomori Prefecture Society for the Promotion of Traditional Martial Arts.[196] Ittō-ryū always took pride of place as the school that most epitomized these ancient martial traditions. It's still passed on that way.

Endnotes to Chapter Six

[160] Tsugaru Nobumasa (津軽信政)

[161] Tsugaru Nobuhisa (津軽信寿)

[162] Okinobu (興信)

[163] *Heigaku* (兵学)

[164] Takami (高美)

[165] Ono Jirōemon Tadayoshi (小野次右衛門忠喜)

[166] Tsugaru Yasuchika (津軽寧親)

[167] Yamada Ichigaku (山田一学)

[168] Yamada Yūzō (山田有蔵)

[169] Takeda Yagaku (武田弥学)

[170] Yamada Kichijiro (山田吉次郎)

[171] Sudō Hanbei Masatake (須藤半兵衛正万)

[172] Masayasu (正安)

[173] Kakizaki Kensuke (柿崎謙助)

[174] Tsugaru Yukitsugu (津軽順承)

[175] Sasamori Teiji (笹森貞司)

[176] Ichinohe Manzō (一戸万蔵)

[177] Honda Kenichi (本多謙一)

[178] Nakahata Hidegorō (中畑英五郎)

[179] Takano Sasaburō (高野佐三郎)

[180] *Densho* (伝書).

[181] Nakanishi Chūta (中西忠太)

[182] Asari Yoshiaki (浅利義明)

[183] Susukida (薄田)

[184] Fukuda (福田)

[185] Takemura (武村)

[186] Kimura (木村)

[187] Ōta (太田)

[188] Osugi (小杉)

[189] Higuchi (樋口)

[190] The exploits of Honda Yoichi are discussed in greater detail in Sasamori Takemi's book, *Bushido and Christianity*.

[191] Yamaoka Tetsutarō (山岡鉄太郎)

[192] Osanai Tatsumaro (小山内達磨)

[193] Tazawa Kumekichi (田沢久米吉)

[194] Sudō Kanichirō (須藤歓一郎)

[195] Andō Taiichi (安藤太一)

[196] *Korai Budō Shinkōkai* (古来武道振興会).

CHAPTER SEVEN

Ittō-ryū Transmission Records

Formalities for Performing the Blood Oath

Those who would like to study Ittō-ryū first call on a good teacher and swear an oath[197] to the gods in heaven and earth that they are joining the school with no ulterior motives, will not slack off in their training, will be loyal students, protect the lessons of the tradition, never showing them or divulging them to others, keep what they learn strictly secret, and never reveal any forms of written material that is bestowed upon them to even their closest family members. The code of Ittō-ryū requires students to affirm these promises in the form of a written oath.

Once they are accepted as students, they follow the instructions of their teachers with sincerity and fidelity, never recklessly engage in duels without permission, nor do anything that would bring discredit upon the school. They must never become a teacher of this school without a license from their master, even if they were to go to another domain or country.

Were they to transgress against this oath, they would be committing an act that would bring the wrath of heaven, so they drew blood from a finger and pledged their lives to keeping this code by making a fingerprint in their own blood as a sign of their sincerity. As those [making the pledge] at the time were of different faiths, they expressed the full depth of their commitment by running through a list of the names of the various gods and bodhisattvas to which they pledged. Examples of the written oaths the author of this book took are below.

Written Oaths

Example One

Written Oath[198]:
- ⊖ I will not show or divulge any of the lessons of Ittō-ryū Heihō to those not permitted to receive them.
- ⊖ I will not engage in duels without permission.
- ⊖ I will never reveal or divulge any of the contents of the secret documents of the school to those who are not permitted to receive them, including even to my parents or other family members.
- ⊖ Regarding the techniques, formalities, and tactics, I will practice them following the instructions of my teacher without any duplicity or ulterior motive.
- ⊖ Even if I were to go to another domain, I would not present myself as a teacher.

I hereby submit that violating the above requires that I accept the punishment of Bonten, Taishaku-ten, the Four Heavenly Kings, the gods of heaven and earth, great, medium, and small, of the more-than-sixty provinces of Japan, especially the two avatars of Izu and Hakone, the Bright Deity of Mishima, the Great

Bodhisattva Hachiman, Tenman Daijizai Tenjin, and in particular the Great Protector Marishiten and the local deities who guard us.

Year, day, month

Name
Blood seal

Example Two

Written Oath:
- I am overjoyed and grateful to receive the teachings of how to wield the sword of Ittō-ryū Heihō. I will never reveal or divulge the contents of what has been handed down to me to those not authorized to receive them.
- I will not engage in duels with other schools or even within our own school without your permission.
- In learning the techniques, formalities, and tactics of this combat system, I bear no malice or duplicity toward my teacher.
- As to learning the sword, I will firmly follow the directions of my teacher and not dilute them by mixing in my own views.
- In the case I would like to transfer to another school, I will present my intention in written form. After receiving approval in writing, I will take it to my next teacher.
- It goes without saying that after I am no longer your student, I will not show or divulge the details of this school to others. Even if I train with others, I will not train in such a way that I will mix in what I have learned from you with the teachings of other schools.

Addendum: I will not present myself as a teacher.

I hereby submit that violating the above requires that I accept the punishment of Bonten, Taishaku-ten, the Four Heavenly Kings, the gods of heaven and earth, great, medium, and small, of the more-than-sixty provinces of Japan, especially the two avatars of Izu and Hakone, the Bright Deity of Mishima, the Great Bodhisattva Hachiman, Tenman Daijizai Tenjin, and in particular the Great Protector Marishiten and the local deities who guard us.

Year, day, month

Name
Blood seal

Record of Transmission within the House of Tsugaru

Nobumasa's Record of Initiation

Ittō-ryū Heihō

Junikajō scroll	A certain auspicious day, April 1686
Kana scroll	A certain auspicious day, June 1686
Hon scroll	A certain auspicious day, May 1689
Wari scroll	December 7, 1689
License	April 7, 1690

All of the above were presented by Ono Jirōemon Tadao.

Seal of Tsugaru Nobumasa

Nobuhisa's Record of Initiation, entry 1

<u>Ittō-ryū Heihō</u>

Junikajō scroll	A certain auspicious day, May 1689
Kana scroll	A certain auspicious day, June 1692
Hon scroll	March 7, 1695
Wari scroll	A certain auspicious day, April 1701

All of the above were presented by Ono Jirōemon Tadao.

Seal of Tsugaru Nobuhisa

Nobuhisa's Record of Initiation, entry 2

To: Lord Tsugaru Nobuhisa

I am happy to inform you of the following.

I, as the third-generation heir of Ittō-ryū Heihō, passed on the entirety of its contents without leaving out a single word or movement. However, the scrolls I gave you will be especially helpful wherever you failed to grasp my lessons or if you happen to forget them. I transmitted the deepest secrets with the greatest care and affection, without leaving anything out. All was transmitted without the slightest omission.

I swear to the gods of Japan the above is true.

May 23

Seal of Ono Jirōemon Tadao

To: Ono Jirōemon Tadao

I am pleased to reply.

This is to express my utmost appreciation on this occasion of receiving the highest-level license of Ittō-ryū Heihō. From this day forward I will teach those who are devoted to Ittō-ryū, but I will never teach in such a way that I show fear or favor to nobility and other high-ranking officials, those in my inner circle, in return for gifts or honorarium, or in pursuit of profit. This is how I will fulfill my oath to my ancestors. By doing the above I will not neglect honoring the gods.

May 23

Seal of Tsugaru Tosa-no-Kami

Nobuhisa's Record of Initiation, entry 3

To: Lord Tsugaru Nobuhisa

Because you have had the utmost devotion to Ittō-ryū Heihō for many years, I have passed on to you the doctrine of the school as handed down to me by my father, as well as all of my own thoughts on the subject, leaving nothing out.

Due to this, you may pass the four scrolls on to those who are [still] deeply devoted to Ittō-ryū Heihō and to those who may have an earnest desire to learn it after ascertaining their true intentions and having them swear an oath.

Since I have completely revealed all of the movements and knowledge that I have, I bestow upon you this license.

With all sincerity.

May 23, 1709

Ono Jirōemon Tadao
Descendent of the Founder, Itō Ittōsai Kagehisa

Nobuhisa's Record of Initiation, entry 4

The situation surrounding this direct transmission of the main line was described in Chapter Five.

Record of Transmission within the House of Yamaga

Takami's Record of Initiation, entry 1

Ittō-ryū Heihō
License to Operate a School with Complete Independence

Age: 44
Yamaga Takami

Takami's Record of Initiation, entry 2

To: Lord Yamaga Hachirōemon

After earnestly training in Ittō-ryū Heihō for many years without fail, you are granted the three scrolls of our school. This was made clear through the record of initiation granted by Nakanishi Tanetake. On this occasion, however, you are taught the inner mysteries of Ittō-ryū directly, with nothing left out. If you don't get confused or get off course, the fruits of Certain Victory will surely be within your grasp.

With all sincerity.

An auspicious day in March, 1788

Seal of Ono Jirōemon Tadayoshi
Commander of Musketeers

Takami's Record of Initiation, entry 3

To: Lord Yamaga Hachirōemon

You are hereby granted permission to open your own training hall. You may take on students who earnestly and

128

truly wish to learn Ittō-ryū. Moreover, since training with bamboo swords could lead one astray, only those who have received the *Junikajō* license and above can train that way as a special exception.

Auspicious day in March, 1790

Seal of Ono Jirōemon Tadayoshi

Takaatsu's Record of Initiation, entry 1

Ittō-ryū Heihō
License to Operate a School with Complete Independence
Received from Ono Jirōemon Tadataka in September 1811.

Age: 37
Yamaga Takaatsu

Takaatsu's Record of Initiation, entry 2

To: Lord Yamaga Jirōsaku

I am happy to inform you of the following.

It has gradually gotten colder, but I would like to express my congratulations on the fact that your efforts are progressing smoothly. The fact is I intend to present to you a license of this school, so I request your presence on the 11th, past nine o'clock, wearing your linen jacket.

Jirōemon said he would like to hear your opinion on the above.
An addendum is attached.

September 10

Written on behalf of Ono Jirōemon:
Nomura Yazaemon
Yamori Naoki

Takaatsu's Record of Initiation, entry 3

To: Lord Yamaga Jirōsaku

From a young age you have tirelessly practiced and been deeply dedicated to Ittō-ryū Heihō. The three scrolls of our school passed on in-house, all awarded by Mr. Nakanishi, are evidence of this. On this occasion, you are hereby granted permission to open your own school. Please take care of, and provide your support to, all of the retainers who are eager to learn. When all is said and done, I ask that you master the doctrine of our school with great care and pass on the essence of Certain Victory.

September, 1811

Seal of Ono Jirōemon Tadayoshi

Takaatsu's Record of Initiation, entry 4

To: Lord Yamaga Jirōsaku

The approach of practicing with the bamboo sword in [the Nakanishi] school is not something you can do easily while remaining true to your blood oath. Therefore, continuing to devote yourself to what you first learned from Nakanishi Chuzō gives the impression that you are devaluing the kata we do during kumitachi training. Because those in your family have a special affinity for the way things are done in that school, you should take care not to let this get out of hand. Moreover, as decided previously, when it comes to how to properly practice with the bamboo sword, you can make a special exception for those who have been bestowed the *Junikajō* license and above. But when it comes to those who are just starting out, you mustn't let them do this useless activity. I say this to leave you with my thoughts on this matter.

[Undated]

Ono Jirōemon

Note: Yamaga Sokō's family lineage. All those listed below use the family name *Yamaga*.[200]

Formal Given Name	Common Name 1	Common Name 2	In the service of:
	Takasuke	Jingozaemon	
Hachirōzaemon	Okinobu (興信)	Daigaku	Tsugaru Nobumasa
Ibid.	Takatoyo	Kennosuke	Nobuhisa
Ibid.	Takanao	Shizuma	Ibid.
Ibid.	Takami	Kosaburō	Ibid.
Jirōsaku	Takaatsu	2nd son of Takami	Ittō-ryū
Tomozō	Takahisa		Tsugaru Yukitsugu
Morie	Takayuki		Ibid.
Motojirō	Takatomo		Tsugaru Tsugiakira

Records of Transmission within the House of Sudō

Scrolls and Licenses

1. *Ittō-ryū Heihō Junikajō* scroll

On August 17, 1812, while stationed in Edo, Sudō Hanbei[201][202] received the above scroll from Nakanishi Inotarō.[203] On February 20, 1844, Sudō Hannomune[204] inherited this scroll. On January 12, 1863, Sudō Saihachi inherited this scroll.

2. *Ittō-ryū Heihō Kana* scroll

On Oct 11, 1820, Sudō Hanbei received the above scroll from Nakanishi Inotarō Tsugumasa. On July 12, 1847, Sudō Hannomune inherited this scroll, and on May 11, 1864, Sudō Saihachi inherited this scroll.

3. *Ittō-ryū Heihō Hon* scroll

On December 27, 1822, while serving his post in Edo, Sudō Hanbei received the above scroll from Nakanishi Inotarō Tsugumasa. On November 17, 1852 Nakanishi Chūbei Tsugumasa conferred the secret documents to Sudō Hannomune. On May 14, 1866, Sudō Saihachi inherited them.

4. *Ittō-ryū Heihō Toritate* License

On November 17, 1852,[205] while serving at his post in Edo, Sudō Hannomune received this license from Nakanishi Chūbei Tsugumasa. On May 14, 1866, Sudō Saihachi inherited this license.

5. *Ittō-ryū Shinan* License

On February 17, 1823, while serving at his post in Edo, Sudō Hanbei received the above certificate from Nakanishi Chūbei, who at the time was serving the household of Okudaira Daizen Taifu. (It was noted in the margin of the *Toritate* license signed by Tsugumasa and dated March 23, 1835, that there was no need to prepare a *Shinanyaku* license because Hanbei already had the *Toritate*.)

6. *Ittō-ryū Tetsujō Tekka* Certificate

On February 17, 1823, Sudō Hanbei received the above license from Nakanishi Chūbei. On November 17, 1852, Sudō Hannomune received the above license from the venerable Nakanishi Chūbei Tsugumasa, who passed away at the age of 73. On May 14, 1866, Sudō Saihachi inherited this.

Ittō-ryū Heihō Poems for Beginners

⊖ Kenjutsu is just like pushing a cart uphill; if you slack off, you will return to where you started.

⊖ In kenjutsu, if you let your guard down, you will die. When it comes to life and death, you should know where you need to focus yourself and where you need not.

⊖ You can wield a long bamboo sword without regard to distance or timing, but you should know that there is a difference when it comes to steel and wooden swords due to their relative heft.

⊖ When you engage with the sword, defend yourself by not becoming fixed in place. Your mind should be calm but your techniques fierce.

⊖ Victory lies in the contest over *aiuchi* [206]– you should know that just poking at your enemy is defeat.

⊖ In execution, you must integrate [lessons contained in] the kumitachi with what you do with the bamboo sword. Principles come out of techniques; techniques come out of principles.

⊖ In kenjutsu, those who are skilled know their own weaknesses; those who are self-satisfied with their own abilities are the unskilled ones.

- You mustn't think of showing the techniques you know to others. Be mindful of what others can see – these techniques are not meant for show.
- It is impossible to put into words the highest applied principles. [207] All you can do is work hard to bring techniques in accord with principle.
- Moving forward is allowed. Retreating is what you are never allowed to do. Make what this means your first principle.
- You might stare death in the face in a crisis, but you should confront the situation with the resolve of being prepared to sacrifice your life; fortune favors the bold.
- There are "high level secrets"[208] in all of the Ways, but these are always carried out with free-flowing spontaneity.[209]

The twelve stanzas above are what you need to know when you do kenjutsu.

Fear, surprise, doubt, and confusion are the "diseases" of the martial arts.

Seal of Sudō Hanbei Masakata

Record of Transmission within the House of Sasamori

(1) Scrolls and Licenses

<u>Ittō-ryū Heihō</u>

Junikajō scroll	May 18, 1922
Kana scroll	June 8, 1924
Hon scroll	April 7, 1926
Wari scroll	April 7, 1926

As mentioned previously, the above were provided by Yamaga
Motojirō Takatomo

Age: 41
Sasamori Junzō

(2) *Toritate*[210] License:

To: Mr. Sasamori Junzō

For many years, starting when you were a child, you
unceasingly worked so hard to master the tactics of
swordsmanship preserved within this house that you
earned great respect and admiration. While eagerly
devoting yourself to your personal development, you
mastered the enduring principles of our school and
surpassed many others to become the [top student].
Therefore, you are awarded this *Toritate* License. If there is
anyone who sincerely desires to learn Ittō-ryū, you may
provide them your full patronage, once you receive their
verbal oath and blood seal as stipulated previously. Never
hinder anyone's progress along the Way. No matter how
well you master the techniques of kenjutsu, you should
revere the inner mysteries[211] of Certain Victory, which is
the inherited wisdom of our ancestors, and must never just
freely give them away.

April 7, 1926

Yamaga Motojirō Takatomo

(3) Tetsujō Tekka[212] License:

To: Sasamori Junzō

Mastering the fundamentals of swordsmanship entails getting to the heart of the four corners and eight directions, the horizontal and vertical, and the above and below [of our school]. This school, which has flowed from Kagehisa, the founder, and coursed through Tadaaki, Tadatsune, Tadao, Tadakazu, Tadakata, Tadayoshi, Takami, Takaatsu, Takahisa, and Takano, follows the immutable principle that governs all things under Heaven and Earth. This is the immutable principle of Yang. In time, Yang transforms into Yin. The beginning is the end and the end is the beginning. It's due to this that you get the return of spring after a cold winter[213]; what comes after moves in accord with what came before. In the end, it is achieving everything you set out to do, leaving nothing undone.

April 7, 1926

Yamaga Motojirō Takatomo

(4) Teaching License[214] *and Official Supplemental Certificates*[215]:

To: Mr. Sasamori Junzō

On this occasion, I am presenting you the *Toritate* license due to your tireless dedication to Ittō-ryū kenjutsu since you were young. From now on, once you confirm that the skill level of those under your patronage is up to par, you may fix your seal to the three documents and bestow them

137

to your students. If they apply themselves even more assiduously under your instruction, you may grant these [supplemental] certificates.

These supplemental certificates are listed below.
⊖ *Habiki*
⊖ *Hosshatō*
⊖ *Junikajō* scroll

April 7, 1926

Yamaga Motojirō Takatomo

Letters, Diagrams, and Other Reference Material

(1) *Certificate of Introduction into the Inner Mysteries of Ittō-ryū.*[216]

To: All of My Students

On this occasion, I couldn't be more honored to pass to you the many inner mysteries passed down to me through successive generations from the founder, Kagehisa, leaving nothing out. And you will bequeath this training to your students. You should discuss these with your students after they start training, even those who may not yet be ready to grasp them. But, as you know, not continually developing your techniques is, above all, juvenilely neglecting to do your utmost. Throw yourself into all areas as you have done up until now, and I ask that you hand these down so that your training will thrive.

But, nowadays, Jirō Saburō, having been the top student of the school for a long time, and being part of the family, has been passed the secrets of the school, so you can consult with him. Teachers and their senior assistants from other schools also rely on him, so you should seek their opinions and train with them too.

From here on, I wait to hear your intentions.

September 17, 1798

Ono Sukekurō

Note: The above letter confirming the transmission of Ittō-ryū's *Kaiden Hirōjō* transcribed by the hand of Jirōemon Tadataka, a descendant of Ono Sukekurō, transmitted the inner secrets passed down from his father, Tadayoshi. It was addressed to Yamaga Hachirōemon Takami, the most senior of his disciples, and listed him as the best of all his students. The lessons within it were disclosed to his students and passed down within the House of Yamaga, generation by generation, until Takatomo, who presented them to me at the same time that I received the full transmission of Ittō-ryū from him.

(2) Notes and memoranda on the kumitachi addressed to Yamaga Hachirōemon [Takami] personally written by Ono Jirōemon Tadayoshi.

(3) Transmission documents,[217] the *Kurai of the Ringing Bell*, a document on the *Five Elements*, as well as a poem provided to Yamaga Hachirōemon Takaatsu written by the hand of Nakanishi Chūta Tsuguhiro.

(4) A painting with a poem written on it by Nakanishi Chūbei Tsugumasa himself on a hanging scroll awarded to Sudō Hanbei along with his full transmission documents.

(5) One volume of *Notebooks*[218] and one copy of *Memoranda* penned by Yamaga Hachirōemon Takaatsu and two of his oaths swearing loyalty to Ittō-ryū.

(6) Training register from the House of Tsugaru during the Tenpō Reign [1830-1844], and student and official teacher enrollment registers of various martial arts within the family.
  ⊖ Student enrollment register listing sixty students of Sudō Hanbei
  ⊖ Student enrollment register listing thirty-six students of Kakizaki Kensuke.

(7) Ittō-ryū's *Ancestral Book of Secrets*[219] from the House of Tsugaru.

Endnotes to Chapter Seven

¹⁹⁷ *Keppan* (血判)

¹⁹⁸ *Kishōmon* (起請文)

¹⁹⁹ The date in the original text is listed as the eighth year of Tenpō (天保八戊申), however, no such date exists, so this is likely a typographical error. The dates that follow all fall within the Tenmei Reign, indicating that the correct date should be the eighth year of Tenmei (天明八戊申), which is 1788.

²⁰⁰ *Yamaga* (山鹿)

²⁰¹ The original text reads Sudō Saihachi, but this is probably a typographical error.

²⁰² Sudō Hanbei Masatake (須藤半兵衛正万)

²⁰³ Nakanishi Inotarō [Tsugumasa] (中西猪太郎)

²⁰⁴ Sudō Hannomune Masayasu (須藤半之極正安)

²⁰⁵ There appears to be a character missing in the text, which makes the exact year impossible to determine; however, the likely date is 1852.

²⁰⁶ *Aiuchi* refers to two people striking each other at the same time.

²⁰⁷ *Riai* (理合)

²⁰⁸ *Gokui* (極意)

²⁰⁹ *Munen-musō* (無念無想)

²¹⁰ *Toritate* (取立)

²¹¹ *Gokui* (極意)

²¹² *Tetsujō Tekka Menjō* (徹上撤下免状)

²¹³ *Ichiyō raifuku* (一陽来復)

²¹⁴ *Shinanyaku menjō* (指南役免状)

²¹⁵ *Origaminin soejō* (折紙認添状)

²¹⁶ *Ittō-ryū Gokui Kaiden Hirōjō* (一刀流極意皆伝披露状)

²¹⁷ *Denshō* (伝書)

²¹⁸ 多与梨草

²¹⁹ *Hidenshō* (秘伝書)

Glossary of Terms

Bakufu: The military government of Japan between 1192 and 1868, headed by the shogun.

Budō: Japanese martial arts.

Daimyo: Lord or vassal of the shogun.

Diet of Japan: Japan's national legislative body.

Densho: Documents that contain information about the techniques, lessons, and philosophical principles of a school of ancient martial arts. These were typically considered secrets of the school and only passed on to the most trusted students.

Edo: The headquarters of the Tokugawa Shogunate, it became the de-facto capital of Japan after 1603. Was later renamed Tokyo.

Fukuro shinai: Practice sword made from slats of split bamboo tied together and covered in a leather or cloth (usually canvas) sheath.

Gekiken (also read as Gekken): A type of contest similar to a duel but with bamboo swords and protective gear. Some sources cite it as the precursor to modern kendo.

Gokui: The philosophical concepts of Ittō-ryū considered the "secrets" of the school.

Hakama: Loose trousers with many pleats on the front, worn as part of formal attire in Japan.

Hatamoto: Direct retainer or vassal of the shogun. Also referred to as *bannermen*.

Heihō: In common usage, this term refers to strategy, tactics, or more generally, the art of war. In a martial arts context, it has become synonymous with skill in swordsmanship. Can also be read as *hyōhō*.

Jōdan posture: Stance in which the sword his held overhead with the sword tip pointing to the rear.

Kata: Prearranged pattern of movement done by practitioners as a means to practice the physical movements of the school as well as instantiate the school's metaphysical concepts.

Keikokan: Training academy for samurai of the Tsugaru Domain established in 1796 by Tsugaru Yasuchika.

Kendo: Japanese form of fencing with two-handed bamboo swords, originally developed as a competitive form of sword training for samurai, but practiced today mainly as a sport.

Kendoka: Someone who practices kendo. A kendo player.

Kenjutsu: Literally *techniques of the sword*, this refers to practical Japanese swordsmanship and fencing extant in Japan before the creation of the sport of kendo. In principle, kenjutsu techniques were designed for use on the battlefield or for personal defense and kenjutsu was a principal weapon system taught in over 2,000 schools in the past. Other names for this include: *tōjutsu, kenpō,* and *tōhō*.

Koku: The amount of rice it took to feed one person for one year in feudal Japan. This metric was generally used to determine the revenue of a feudal domain.

Kumitachi: The full collection of all of the physical techniques of Ittō-ryū. The kumitachi is subdivided into discreet sequences of moves called *kata*.

Kurai: In the context of Ittō-ryū, *kurai* refers to specialized tactics, techniques, or procedures.

Makimono: A scroll that typically contained a list of techniques or lessons. It serves as a license.

Musōken: One of the highest secrets of Ittō-ryū, this refers to moving in response to your opponent without conscious thought.

Naginata: Japanese halberd.

Onigote: Large gloves with thick forearm protection worn in training as protective gear.

Rōnin: A samurai with no lord or master.

Seigan posture: Stance in which the sword is held to the front with the tip at eye level.

Shikata: In paired training, shikata assumes the role of the junior partner and executes techniques against uchikata, the senior partner.

Shinai: Practice sword with a blade made from split bamboo strips tied together.

Shinai Kyougi: Name given to an offshoot of kendo practiced immediately after the end of WWII in which combatants wore Western-style fencing equipment and used modified rules in order to circumvent the prohibition on kendo imposed by the U.S. occupation authorities. Sometimes referred to as *pliant-stick fighting,* the direct translation of Shinai Kyougi.

Sōke: The headmaster of a traditional school of Japanese martial arts. Also, the title given to the headmasters of other traditional arts in Japan, such as the tea ceremony, flower arranging, and others.

Too-Gijuku: Secondary educational school founded in 1872 by Honda Yoichi and Kukichi Kuro when they reconstructed the Tsugaru Domain's training academy, the Keikokan, as a private school. The Too-Gijuku exists today as the Too-Gijuku Junior-Senior High School.

Uchikata: In paired training, uchikata assumes the role of the senior partner who teaches his junior partner, shikata, how to perform the school's techniques.

Wakigamae posture: Stance in which the sword is held to one's side with the tip pointing toward the ground.

Yamaga-ryū: A school of military strategy developed and taught by Yamaga Sokō and his descendants.

Sources Cited

A Source Book in Chinese Philosophy. Translated and edited by Wing-Tsit Chan. Princeton: Princeton University Press, 1963.

Confucius. *The Spring and Autumn Annals (Shunjū Sashiden)*. N.p. [thought to have been written 722-481 BCE and edited by Confucius later.]

Hall, David A. *Encyclopedia of Japanese Martial Arts*. New York: Kodansha USA, Inc. 2012.

Lao Tzu. *Classic of the Way and its Virtue (Tao-te ching)*. N.p. [thought to have been written between 400 BCE and 200 BCE.]

Ō no Yasumaru. *Record of Ancient Matters (Kojiki)*. N.p. [thought to have been written circa 711-712 AD].

Ōe no Masafusa. *Tōsenkyō* (闘戦経). N.p, [thought to have been written circa 1100].

Robin McNeal. *Conquer and Govern: Early Chinese Military Texts from the Yizhou Shu*. Honolulu: University of Hawaii Press, 2012.

Sasamori Junzō. *Kendo*. Tokyo: Obunsha, 1955.

Sasamori Junzō and Gordon Warner. *This is Kendo: The Art of Japanese Fencing*. North Clarendon VT: Charles E. Tuttle Co. Inc., 1964.

Sasamori Takemi. *Bushido and Christianity*. Translated by Mark Hague. Tokyo: Reigakudō Press, 2016.

About the Author

Sasamori Junzō (1886-1976) is perhaps most well-known in Japan's martial arts community for his work in keeping the U.S. occupation authorities under General Douglas MacArthur from completely banning the practice of kendo. His efforts placed him in the annals of Japanese history as one of the saviors of Japan's martial arts. His life was much more than just the martial arts, however. He worked as a reporter for newspapers and political magazines in Japan and the U.S., served as the chancellor of two educational institutions, was a statesman who served in the legislature, the cabinet, and ministerial posts for over two decades, and founded his own Christian church in Tokyo. Born into a samurai family a little over a decade after the samurai class was abolished, Junzō was a key link between the modern world and Japan's samurai past.

About the Translator

Mark Hague's martial arts career has spanned over 42 years, 19 of which in Japan, and he holds dan rankings in several styles of karate and aiki-jujitsu. He started training in Ono-ha Ittō-ryū in the Reigakudō under Sasamori Takemi in 2002 and was awarded the *Kanajisho* license in 2009. He continues to practice Ono-ha Ittō-ryū under the current sōke, Yabuki Yūji. His previous translations include *Bushido and Christianity*, by Sasamori Takemi.

Printed in Great Britain
by Amazon

42658777R00106